P9-AFD-311

beatgeneration

Glory Days in Greenwich Village

The mountain bear has a hole in his pants--trouble.
Doctors get free passes to my museum
in return for their lobatomies on me.
I am not afraid to work--I would love to fly a dirigable.
Nor am I afraid to be a colector of lamps--
provided everyone help me.
And as for your cantelopes, 2/for29--I consider it dangerous.
My fortune is dedicated to going to see movies.
I dont go anywhare without my belt,
cause I own everything that lays inside my belt.
And when ever theres a man on the corner
telling me theres a boat leaving for heaven now,
I'll go & never speak another word.

There was this fellow I was telling you about
who built somthing in his room,he built & built
untill it got too big for his room,then he had to move
then he always had to move, that was him.
Then this new follow who went out to the store
and he walked & he walked,and one block went behind him,
then another,then another ahead & that went behind him
& so on till he was far away from home--
all because of the way sombody said somthing on T.V.

O science give me twenty feet
twenty Grandma meat ball eyes
take me apart in the robot room
just give me one thing extraordinary
(I got somthing going here now,
    dont rush me,I got this typewritter, right
    got this paper here, right
    all alone, right--)   spelT
Walking over to put music on phnograph space,
bringing cover(of composer) back to desk to see hows it spelt--
Pictures at Exhibition by Musorsky   but this room is all alone
                                         with too much of myself in it.
But yet,how much beauty has rolled off the breast of a dying swan
that lay cooling on the grass wile the Host is shaving its shadow? x

                                    Peter Orlovsky

beatgeneration

Glory Days in Greenwich Village

FRED W. McDARRAH
GLORIA S. McDARRAH

SCHIRMER BOOKS
AN IMPRINT OF SIMON & SCHUSTER MACMILLAN • NEW YORK

PRENTICE HALL INTERNATIONAL
LONDON MEXICO CITY NEW DELHI SINGAPORE SYDNEY TORONTO

© 1996 Fred W. McDarrah and Gloria S. McDarrah
Photographs © 1996 Fred W. McDarrah

Grateful acknowledgment and thanks is given to the following poets and/or their literary
agents, estates, or publishers, for the reprinting of the original manuscripts that appear
throughout this book:

"Untitled Poem," © by Peter Orlovsky. From *Clean Asshole Poems & Smiling Vegetable Songs*.
    © 1978, Northern Lights, Crono, ME.
"For My Annie" by Brigid Murnaghan, courtesy the author.
"Billie Holliday, 1959" by Robert Losada, courtesy the author.
"C o u p l e t s" by Paul Blackburn from *The Collected Poems of Paul Blackburn*, ©1958, 1985
    by Joan Blackburn. Reprinted by permission of Persea Books, Inc.
"Upside Down" by Barbara Guest, courtesy the author.
"Back of Town Blues" by Jack Micheline, © 1969 Yellow Horn-Golden Mountain Press 1975, Streets
    of Lost Fools Streets Press 1975.
"Nocturne" by Diane di Prima. "Nocturne" is in *Freddie Poems*, Eidolon Editions, © 1974 by Diane
    di Prima. All rights reserved.
"I Beg You Come Back & Be Cheerful" by Allen Ginsberg, © Allen Ginsberg. Allen Ginsberg's poetry is
    published by Harper/Collins Inc., 10 E. 53rd St., New York, NY 10022.
"Rhythm" by Jimmy Lyons, courtesy the author.
"Playmates Future Laymates" by Ted Joans,
    courtesy the author.
"This Is a Poem by Albert Saijo Lew Welch and Jack Kerouac" by Albert Saijo, Lew Welch,
    and Jack Kerouac. © The Estate of Stella Kerouac, John Sampas Literary Rep. 1996;
    Albert Saijo, and Lew Welch, courtesy Grey Fox Press.
"Open Letter to *Life* Magazine" by William Burroughs, © 1996 by William Burroughs.
"TRAIN TRIP U.S.A." by Daisy Aldan, courtesy the author.
"Excerpts from The Anonymous Diary of a New York Youth" by Taylor Mead, courtesy the author.
"Poem" by Frank O'Hara, © Frank O'Hara, from *Collected Poems* by Frank O'Hara, courtesy Alfred
    A. Knopf Incorporated.
"how pussy cats manage to swing" by Ray Bremser, courtesy the author; marginal comments by
    Jack Kerouac, © The Estate of Stella Kerouac, John Sampas Literary Rep. 1996.
"Greenwich Village of My Dreams" by Tuli Kupferberg, courtesy the author.
"Pot" by Gregory Corso, courtesy the author.
"Loud Prayer" by Lawrence Ferlinghetti, courtesy the author.
"poem for a girl i booted" by William Morris, courtesy Marlene Morris.
"The Physical World" by Amiri Baraka, courtesy the author.
"The Shape of Death" by May Swenson, used with permission of The Literary Estate of May Swenson.
Beatnik Magazine parody from *Mad* magazine, September 1960. Copyright by E.C. Publications Inc.
    Reprinted by permission of William Gaines, *Mad* magazine.

All rights reserved. No part of this book may be reproduced or transmitted in any form or
by any means, electronic or mechanical, including photocopying, recording, or by any
information storage and retrieval system, without permission in writing from the Publisher.

Schirmer Books
An Imprint of Simon & Schuster Macmillan
1633 Broadway
New York, NY 10019

Library of Congress Catalog Card Number: 96–7592

Printed in the United States of America

Printing Number

1 2 3 4 5 6 7 8 9 10

Library of Congress Cataloging in Publication Data

McDarrah, Fred W., 1926 –
    Beat generation: glory days in Greenwich Village/Fred W. McDarrah, Gloria S. McDarrah
    p. cm
    Includes bibliographical references and index.
    ISBN: 0–02–864593–6
    1. Beat generation—Pictorial works. 2. Authors, American—20th Century—Portraits.
3. Greenwich Village (New York, N.Y.)—Social life and customs—Pictorial works. 4. Authors,
American—20th Century—Homes and haunts—New York (N.Y.)—Pictorial works. 5. Kerouac, Jack,
1922–1969—Friends and associates—Portraits. I.
McDarrah, Gloria S. II. Title
PS228.B6M42 1996
810.9'0054—dc20
                           96–7592
                            CIP

This paper meets the requirements of ANSI/NISO Z39.48–1992 (Permanence of Paper).

preface

It's hard to remember today how outrageous the Beats were when the movement was new. Jack Kerouac's picture wasn't being used in advertisements to sell men's clothing; he (and his work) were almost universally derided, by literary critics and the public at large. Besides small groups of like-minded souls in a few enclaves in major cities—primarily New York's Greenwich Village where we lived—there were few people who would admit to being "Beat," and even among the Beats themselves there were healthy arguments about exactly what the term meant. It was a radical statement to proclaim yourself a member of this fraternity, at a time in American life when radicals were universally shunned.

The public believed that a Beatnik was anybody who looked scruffy, carried a sheaf of crumpled pages, and read a kooky poem that included some four-letter words. The typical Beatnik portrayed in the media never washed, slept in his clothes on the floor on dirty mattresses, begged for money, and was akin to Bowery hobos. When the (supposed) "private lives" of the Beats were exposed, the public was startled and outraged. Fearing these wild creatures had been turned loose to undermine and destroy the public's morals, the media, especially *Time* and *Life* magazines, launched an unprecedented blitz against the Beat Generation, each week alerting the public to the menace. This is a typical outburst from *Time*: "The bearded, sandaled beat likes to be with his own kind, to riffle through his quarterlies, write craggy poetry, paint crusty pictures and pursue his never ending quest for the ultimate in sex and protest. When deterred from such pleasures by the goggle-eyed from Squaresville, the beatnik packs his pot (marijuana), shorts and bongo drums, grabs his blackhosed pony-tailed beatchick and cuts out."

The public never took the Beat Generation seriously, but the Beats in fact were the harbingers of great changes in the United States. They paved the way for the New Journalism of Tom Wolfe, Pete Hamill, Jack Newfield, Hunter Thompson, and Gloria Steinem that was to emerge a decade later. Their love of jazz introduced this music to mainstream America; their interest in Eastern philosophy would encourage an entire generation to look beyond traditional American Puritanism. African-Americans, women, and homosexuals were all prominent members of the Beat movement, and were all treated as equals. The Beats contributed greatly to the cultural change that was to come in the 1960s, and everyone from Hippies to Yippies (to today's Yuppies) has been influenced by their outlook.

This book is not just a nostalgic memoir of a distant time; many of the photos look like they could have been taken just last week in New York. The Beats truly represented the most forward-thinking members of the community; their attitudes, clothing, lifestyles, words, and images have become a part of our national consciousness. I was fortunate to be there at the beginning; I was also fortunate to be interested in documenting a scene that many others disparaged. This book is an homage to these creative artists who I was lucky to admire and to briefly know.

I was born and raised in Brooklyn, where I lived until I was drafted in World War II. After the war, I returned to New York's Greenwich Village. In May of 1948, I photographed my first artist at the Greenwich Village Outdoor Art Show; I then photographed William H. Littlefield in his studio during the summer of 1949. Littlefield, a Boston-born painter who had been in Paris

CONTENTS

in the 1920s and studied with the legendary Hans Hofmann in Provincetown, provided a unique opportunity for outsiders like me to view the inner workings of the art scene. Through Littlefield, I met other members of the New York School, and began hanging out with them at the Cedar Street Bar, a local watering hole that also attracted musicians and writers. I first attended a meeting of the members-only organization founded by the artists themselves, known only as The Club, on November 30, 1956, for a memorial symposium on the recently deceased artist, Jackson Pollock; when Littlefield became The Club's "administrator," taking attendance and folding chairs

William H. Littlefield.

after the meetings, he invited me to be his assistant. The Club guru, Philip Pavia, allowed me to occasionally take a few photos, which he later published in his historic *It Is* magazine. These were the first pictures I ever published. In 1958, Pavia invited me to be The Club's doorman, to make sure only members and their guests were admitted to meetings.

In the late 1950s, there weren't the divisions between writers, dancers, poets, and musicians that there are today. Those in the "avant garde"—or anyway those who thought of themselves as being in the avant garde—grouped together, living in the same neighborhoods, supporting each other's work by attending concerts, openings, readings, and hanging out together. Once I became friendly with the artists, meeting musicians and poets was easy, and soon I was documenting the entire scene.

One reason that artists and writers were attracted to the Village was that rents were cheap. I lived at 304 West 14th Street on the edge of the Village and paid $46.68 a month. In 1960, my then-girlfriend Gloria Schoffel and I moved to 64 Thompson Street, between Spring and Broome, in what is now trendy Soho. We paid $55.57 per month for five rooms and a bath. I sometimes earned about $50 a week, but we could eat out for $2.00. Entertainment was cheap, too: A glass of beer at the Cedar was only a quarter.

Another attraction was that Greenwich Village was truly a "village," a small town within the large city of New York. On weekends, all of Greenwich Village congregated in Washington Square Park to be part of the scene: Norman Mailer, Anatole Broyard, Tuli Kupferberg, Sylvia Topp, Nat Hentoff, Mark Sufrin, Dan List, Harriet Sohmers, Bill Ward, Gil Millstein, Howard Smith, Jack Micheline, Lenny Horowitz, and (of course) Ted Joans. Everybody knew everybody, and it was like a family get-together. Painting, poetry, music, dance, and off-Broadway theater were all in full swing; abstract painters threw globs of paint on canvases; poets shouted Beat words at enthralled cafe crowds. Everybody was "creating" something, and no one deliberately set out to attract media attention. In those years the park was positively quaint, with the Shanty Boys playing their homemade instruments, and people folk danced around the Arch.

Folk dancers in Washington Square Park.

Not that everyone looked on Washington Square as the ideal place for outdoor happenings. It's hard to believe, but in the 1950s it was against the law to read poetry or play a folksong in the park. I guess the police didn't like to see the large crowds of "undesirables" that such behavior attracted. Poet William Morris was thrown into jail for daring to break this rule in 1959 when he gave an impromptu reading. In the early 1960s, the entire community gathered at the park to protest this ridiculous prohibition, and finally folksingers, orators, and poets won their right to perform in the park.

I was an intellectuals' groupie at heart. In the early 1950s I went regularly to the Poetry Center of the YMHA on 92nd Street and heard all the established writers and poets. When the Beat Generation arrived, I was prepared for the onslaught: I admired their work, collected it, read it, and followed their footsteps, going everywhere and taking candid snapshots along the way with an ancient Rolleicord, and later with a well-used 35 mm Nikon S2. I wanted to be part of the action. My camera was my diary, my ticket of admission, my way of remembering, preserving, and proving that I had been there when it all happened.

What really set me apart from the others was that I had a daytime job on the *Village Voice*, a recently started alternative weekly newspaper that thumbed its nose at the establishment and told its small world all about the radical, crazy Beat Generation. In the paper's early days of the 1950s, each issue ran about twelve pages, with articles discussing art, poetry, music, film, dance, and the avant garde. Since I had worked on Madison Avenue in advertising, I became the *Voice*'s space salesman, selling one-inch ads to small local shops and restaurants. At night and on weekends I turned into a demon Beat with a camera, eventually publishing my photos in the paper. Later, editor Dan Wolf, whom I had known since 1949, made me the staff photographer.

While my daytime hours were occupied with the routine task of peddling ads, my other life was far more interesting. Here is an entry from my journal for March 16, 1959: "Met Gloria at Dody Müller's exhibit at the Hansa Gallery. Kerouac, Ginsberg, Corso, Frank, Amram, everybody was there. It was an exciting opening and I took two rolls of pictures. Spoke to Robert Frank about showing his Kerouac film, *Pull My Daisy*, at the Artist's Club. Later Gloria and I had a sandwich at my house and then we went to the Living Theatre to hear Kenneth Patchen read to the jazz of Charlie Mingus. A nice crowd showed up and I took pictures as usual. From there we went to the Cedar Street Tavern and sat in a booth with Ted Joans, Lenny Horowitz, Jack Micheline and William Morris. We drank beer and goofed until 3 A.M. and then went home."

One of the great things about the Beat crowd was that everyone had a sense of fun, whether it was in throwing spontaneous parties or in writing outrageous poems full of nonsense words and rhymes. I was able to join in on the fun when I ran an advertisement in the classified section of the *Voice* for a "Rent-A-Beatnik" service. I was surprised when I was deluged with requests, as well as notes from volunteer Beatniks, to serve as party givers. The result was unintentional national attention—and even a parody "Rent-A-Square" advertisement in *Mad* magazine!

As the months rolled by, I accumulated a lot of photos; some were out-of-focus, blurred, overexposed, underexposed. As a novice photographer I actually threw away some of the negatives that didn't look good. But I had enough material for a book and started to collect poems from everybody. I had met Jack Kerouac at the 1958 New Year's Eve party held at The Club, where I took the now-famous photograph of him holding a small doll.

Fred W. McDarrah (center, with dark glasses and black cap), during his days as a Rent-A-Beatnik entrepreneur, being interviewed by reporter Danny Meenan for Mike Wallace's documentary on the Beat Generation, April 30, 1960.

Kerouac was happy to help with my Beat anthology, contributing a spontaneous poem that he wrote in my 14th Street tenement flat, along with two friends who had accompanied him from California. Other Beats would send poems they had published or written, and I included these along with my photographs of the scene. In 1960 Ted Wilentz of the Eighth Street Bookshop published my book, *The Beat Scene*.

Unlike the artists of the same period, whose goal was to get an uptown show, the poets were more interested in reading their work to anyone who would listen, on the street, in their "pads" (the then-current slang name for an apartment), in the cafes, nightclubs, small theaters, anywhere, including a Bowery cafeteria and an abandoned waterfront pier. They wanted to be visible, admired, heard, and loved. They all had something to say, because they were the first of the postwar generation that rebelled against society. Most of them grew up during the Depression, just as I did. Many had gone to college, served in World War II, and came home to find nothing had changed. In the 1950s, they believed they were chosen to engage in the holy crusade to raise the public consciousness, to "tell the truth," to espouse the philosophy of living to their true feelings, stripping the mask of hypocrisy from a culture long weighed down by the traditional dogma of family, church, and state.

In New York City, the Beat movement lasted only a few years. By the mid-1960s, Village cafes began to feature folk singers, and the bars were jammed with tourists searching for Beatniks. Many writers and poets moved to the West Coast; some went back to school, a few went to prison, others gave up the fight and disappeared. The *Voice* no longer published stories about the Beats.

And our days as Beatniks ended. The scene changed; Franz Kline died, the Artist's Club closed, and the Cedar Tavern burned down. I began to photograph the hippies and peace demonstrations, rock 'n' roll stars, and Andy Warhol's Factory scene. I opened up a bank account and even bought insurance. Gloria and I married, raised two sons, put them through college, became grandparents, produced a dozen books, and bought a cottage in the country. I had settled down at the *Village Voice*, where I have been now for more than 35 years. We're part of the establishment, but I'll never admit it.

It has been over four decades since Jack Kerouac's *On the Road* was written. Numerous friends and my sons, Timothy and Patrick, said it was now time to pull out my photos, many never before published, and do a new book in response to renewed interest in the Beat Generation. Contacting all the writers and poets for biographical sketches was a formidable task. I wanted to find out where they were now, what they had been doing all these years. Finding them years later meant numerous phone calls and letters to friends of friends. The remarkable thing is that everybody I located acted as though we had seen and talked to each other the day before; there seemed to be no distance imposed by the intervening years. Conversations just resumed where they left off.

When the Whitney Museum opened its 1995 show honoring the Beat Generation and its creators, I was pleased to have my photographs selected to help represent the movement. There was only room for a handful of images in the show, so I was especially pleased to be able to present almost 250 of these images in this book, many reproduced for the first time (in fact, I had never *printed* some of these photos before!). I never viewed them as works of art, but rather as documents; they were my attempt to capture a fleeting moment. Looking at the photographs, I see members of the Beat Generation as they were, young, proud, talented—frozen in time— and I remember how it was then, a lifetime ago.

Fred W. McDarrah

acknowledgments

In the time we have spent doing the research and writing for this book, we have been aided by the friendship and support of a great many people, who have all given generously of their time, advice, and expertise. We are grateful for the opportunity to thank some of them here: Donald Allen, David Amram, Lester Blackiston, Karen Braziller, Gregory Corso, Diane di Prima, Lawrence Ferlinghetti, Charles Henri Ford, Allen Ginsberg, James Grauerholz, Bill Hooper, Edie Jarolim, Ted Joans, Rick Kaufmann, Brenda Knight, Rozanne Knudsen, Tuli Kupferberg, Joe Le Sueur, Bob Lubin, David McReynolds, Maureen Morris, Steven Morrison, Brigid Murnaghan, Kenneth P. Norwick, Maureen O'Hara, Bruno Palmer-Poroner, Lisa Phillips, George Plimpton, Jenelle Porter, George Preston, Bob Rosenthal, Barney Rosset, John Sampas, Ann Schwertley, Hy Shore, Jose Garcia Villa, Joan Ward, Ted Wilentz, Charlene Woodcock, and Dorothy Zolkwer.

We give special thanks to Michael Cohen, Randy Mandelbaum, and Eddie Sollinger of New York Film Works.

And, finally, we are indebted to Richard Carlin, of Schirmer Books/Macmillan, for his good advice and guidance throughout this project.

Gloria S. McDarrah
Fred W. McDarrah

FOR MY ANNIE

DANCE YOUR WILD JIG MY
    LOVE

FOR THEN AND ONLY THEN
    I CAN KNOW

THE SORROW AND THE JOY
OF ███ KNOWING

WHAT MY YOUTH WAS FOR.

Brigid Murnaghan
Nov. 15, 1959

yes

anatomyofabeatnik

Scratch a beard... find a Beatnik. It doesn't even make any difference whether you're actually a rabbi, a university professor, a concert musician, a real, live honest to goodness poet, a grocery clerk, or a bus driver. The beard symbol has become so strong that it doesn't matter what or who you are. If you've got a beard, you're a Beatnik.

This symbol system has become such a "thing" in this country that nobody knows what to believe anymore, perhaps because nobody cares; everybody wants the fake, the phony, the spurious anyway. Here's a classic description of America's Beatnik taken from a major Negro magazine: "...Unwashed, bearded, free-loving, pseudo-intellectual, reefer-smoking, nonworking, self-styled artists or writers living in protest of something or other."

Time magazine says Beatniks are "a pack of oddballs who celebrate booze, dope, sex and despair." The same magazine calls Allen Ginsberg "the discount-house Whitman of the Beat Generation." They also call Jack Kerouac the "latrine laureate of Hobohemia."

Time's poison pen sister, another four-letter-word magazine, was perhaps more successful in twisting the pliable minds of Americans. Last fall it published an incendiary piece called "The Only Rebellion Around." It was written by staff writer Paul O'Neil, who is apparently mixed up with fruit flies since he used the expression five times in one paragraph.

Carried away by College Composition I

and II, O'Neil opened his remarkably twisted tale by saying: "If the United States today is really the biggest, sweetest endmost succulent casaba eery produced by the melon patch of civilization, it would seem only reasonable to find its surface profaned—as indeed it is—by a few fruit flies. But reason would also anticipate contented fruit flies, blissful fruit flies, fruit flies raised by happy environment to the highest stages of fruit fly development. Such is not the case. The grandest casaba of all, in disconcerting fact, has incubated some of the hairiest, scrawniest and most discontented specimens of all time: The improbable rebels of the Beat Generation, who not only refuse to sample the seeping juices of American plenty and American social advances but scrape their feelers in discordant scorn of any and all who do."

The illustration of the "well-equipped pad," which accompanied the *Life* feature by O'Neil was so funny it was offensive. I happen to know the girl who posed for the photograph. I'm sure she needed the model fee. She is married to a struggling painter. Both are good people who mind their own business. Their two children are just about the most attractive kids anyone could imagine. Nevertheless, in the illustration she is pegged as "the beat chick dressed in black" surrounded by "naked light bulbs, a hot plate for warming espresso coffee pot and bean cans, a coal stove for heating baby's milk, drying chick's leotards and displaying crucifix-shaped Mexican cow bells." The real killer remark was "a beat baby, who has gone to sleep on

This article was written by Fred W. McDarrah and originally published in Saga, August 1960.

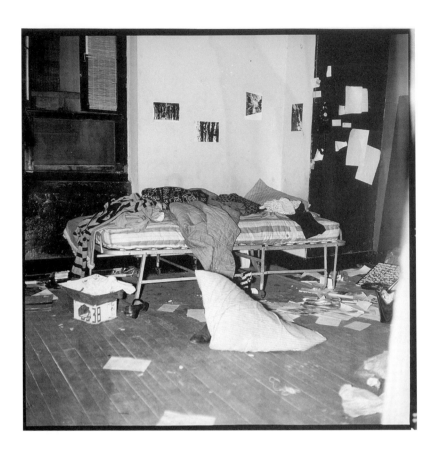

Artist-poet
William Morris's
Beatnik pad,
212 Sullivan Street,
May 24, 1959.

the floor after playing with beer cans." You can imagine how that went over in Dubuque.

Gilbert Millstein of the *New York Times* told me, "We're the innocents." And I guess he's right. How incredibly innocent we must be to be not only fooled but also taken. O'Neil's *Life* article went on and on with cheap drivel, lies, phony stories, misquotes, slander and slaughter of some of my best friends. An apology for a malicious misquote between Allen Ginsberg and Dame Edith Sitwell did not appear in the magazine's Letters column until seven weeks after the original article was published.

Let me use just one more example of how this erroneous impression of the Beat Generation is perpetuated. Last winter the poetry editor of the *Saturday Review*, John Ciardi, wrote about the Beat Generation as "not only juvenile but certainly related to juvenile delinquency through a common ancestor whose best name is Disgust. The street gang rebellion has gone for blood and violence. The Beats have found their kicks in an intellectual pose, in drugs (primarily marijuana but also Benzedrine, mescaline, peyote, assorted goofballs, and occasionally heroin) and in wine, Zen, jazz, sex, and carefully mannered jargon...."

"The Beats wear identical uniforms. They raise nearly identical beards.... They practice an identical aversion to soap and water. They live in the same dingy alleys. They sit around in the same drab dives listening to the same blaring jazz with identical blanked-out expressions on their identical faces. And any one of them would sooner cut his throat than be caught doing anything 'square...'."

It seems clear that the mighty U.S. press has caught on its journalistic meat hook a new scapegoat, a whipping boy, a real live sucker, the so-called Beatnik. It doesn't matter if the facts are straight, after all, we need a little entertainment anyway. The hell with the Truth and down with the Facts. It's better to lay it on the Beatniks than to reflect too seriously on the headlines in the morning paper:

Whites Buy Out Gun Shop As Race Rift Widens in Africa ... City to Intensify Battle on Crime ... House Expands Inquiry into Federal Power Commission and Gas Industry ... Child Kidnapped, Abductors Ask $100,000 ... Militia Aids Castro in Hunt for Rebels ... New Haven Asks Another Fare Increase ... Mistress Stabs Wealthy Sales Executive ....

I could go on and on. Allen Ginsberg puts it much better than I can. "Life is a nightmare for most people, who want something else.... People want a lesser fake of Beauty.... We've seen Beauty face to face, one time or another and said, 'Oh my God, of course, so that's what it's all about, no wonder I was born and had all those secret weird feelings!' Maybe it was a moment of instantaneous perfect stillness in some cow patch in the Catskills when the trees suddenly came alive like a Van Gogh painting or a Wordsworth poem. Or a minute listening to, say, Wagner on the phonograph when the music sounded as if it was getting nightmarishly sexy and alive, awful, like an elephant calling far away in the moonlight."

What Allen describes here are a few basic necessities of life, the things that make us what we are, Truth, Love and Beauty. As I see it there is very little else in the world that means anything. And this is what the real meaning of the Beat Generation is. This is what the so-called Beatnik wants. The Beat wants his life to mean something to himself. He is looking for an Order. Whether he finds it in poetry, painting, music, plumbing, carpentry, weight-lifting, selling shoes, or no matter what, he must find meaning for his life.

Allen Ginsberg and Jack Kerouac at the opening of Dody Müller's (who was then Kerouac's girl-friend) exhibition at the Hansa Gallery, March 16, 1959.

He wants a hero he can genuinely believe in, not like the figure all too frequently presented today, a hero in the form of a professional soldier who won the Bronze Star and half a dozen battle stars, a soldier who carries in his wallet a souvenir photograph of a Red Chinese soldier he bayoneted.

Essentially, it's a matter of living, of awareness, of sensitivity to nature... that single miracle ingredient of life that is present when you stand on top of a hill and face the sunny sky and want to scream at the top of your lungs how wonderful it is to be alive.

The trouble is, most people don't have time for such luxuries of the spirit. They're too mixed up, as Jack Kerouac says, in "hustling forever for a buck among themselves... grabbing, taking, giving, sighing, dying, just so they could be buried in those awful cemetery cities beyond Long Island City."

In deciding what he is pursuing, Jack writes, in his fine book, *On the Road*, "...they danced down the streets like dingledodies, and I shambled after as I've been doing all my life after people who interest me because the only people for me are the mad ones, the ones who are mad to live, mad to talk, mad to be saved, desirous of everything at the same time, the ones who never yawn or say a commonplace thing, but burn, burn, burn like fabulous Roman candles exploding like spiders across the stars...."

I talked to my friend Edwin Fancher about Beatniks and the Beat Generation as we were driving out to Brooklyn to a Methodist church where they were holding a Convocation of Youth. The theme was Man's Strength, Man's Distress. The program consisted of the Beat film *Pull My Daisy*, a lecture on "What Is the Beat Generation?" and a poetry reading by LeRoi Jones, the editor of *Yugen*, which is a pocket-sized literary magazine publishing many Beat writers. The lecture was to be given by Ed.

I first met Ed Fancher at a party nearly a dozen years ago on a snowy New Year's Eve. He was

Ted Joans posing in his raccoon coat at his 4 Astor Place loft, November 4, 1959.

living in the Village and going to the New School for Social Research. He is about 36, a veteran of the war in Europe, has always worn a beard and is a practicing psychologist. Five years ago he started a weekly newspaper in Greenwich Village, *The Village Voice*.

Fancher says that "it is a movement of protest. The Beat looks at the world we live in, everything that is part of our way of life, including finding out what is holy…. They live in a world gone mad and no one cares but them. Not only is the Beat Generation interested in intellectual work, they themselves are very social people. It's an attempt to cry out that what we need is a sense of society. If it's necessary to be part of a crazy, offbeat group, all right, that's better than being detached.

"I think the Beats have achieved popularity in America because they correspond to a very deep sense of unrest in America. Americans don't want to think about the real issues of concern; they want to stick their heads in the sand and avoid anything important. They forget that the Beat Generation does feel it's better to have vitality than to be dead at the core like the rest of America. Many Americans are dead at the core and don't know it. The Beats are interested in religion because they live in a society where no one is interested in it. They live in a hostile society and they are struggling to find the meaning of life outside of that dead society."

The religious theme that Ed Fancher talks about was brought up again by Howard Hart. I don't think it makes much difference that he's a Catholic. I've known Howard for about ten years, from the days when the up-and-coming literary set and the *Catholic Worker* crowd used to hang out in the White Horse Tavern and swill down steins of half 'n' half. Howard has been a drummer and has been writing poetry for a great many years. He's the same age as I and is represented in my picture book *The Beat Scene*. Howard says this about the Beat Generation:

"It's an obvious manifestation of the fact that the whole structure of American life is phony. The clothes and the manner immediately call attention to them [the Beats] because they are declaring something which is really a fact and they want to proclaim it. More than protest, there is an affirmative thing there… they are really looking for God… and after all, God is love. If they didn't have so much of a longing for God in their hearts they wouldn't come on so strong. It's a real search that gives them a kind of right to flaunt themselves even when they haven't got the talent or anything…."

Bernard Scott is another who has some interesting comments to offer. Bud is 31 and is the associate minister of Judson Memorial Church in the heart of Greenwich Village. The church has an adjoining art gallery and sponsors a literary magazine called *Exodus*, which Bud edits. He says, "I always use the term Beatnik to designate a kind of part-time, imitation Bohemianism that was brought up to date with the Beat Generation. The definition of Beatniks rose out of the Beat Generation. It's really nothing more than a couple of dozen writers who helped to define what was happening to people consciously. In fact I remember when I was going to school right after the second war, I was hitchhiking across the country and doing all kinds of weird things. And when the Beat writers came on the scene, I found they were defining me and talking about the things I knew for the first time. They were the articulate spokesmen. I don't associate myself with the Beat Generation in an orthodox, stylistic sense any more, but I welcomed what I saw. They described experiences I knew and they were the first writers to do it.

"When you meet a Beat at a Village party he never asks you what you do because he's not interested in your economic definition. But what you do is one of the first questions you are asked on the outside. Our culture defines people in terms of their utility. The Beat wants to know what you are thinking, what's ticking inside of you, how real you are in your heart, what you've got to say, can you help me see anything, can you turn me on…?"

Somewhat apart from the Beats are the Hipsters, devotees of a philosophy best expressed by Norman Mailer, the author of *The Naked and the Dead*.

I see Norman around the *Village Voice* newspaper office quite a bit since he was one of the paper's founders, and I frequently run into him at parties. At one party I heard him being interviewed for a Monitor radio broadcast so his comments on Hip were abbreviated:

"I would say that Beat is more idyllic than Hip; it assumes that finally all you have to do is relax and find yourself and you'll find peace and honesty with it. Hip assumes that the danger of the modern world is that whenever anyone relaxes that is precisely the moment when he is ambushed. So, Hip is more than a philosophy of ambition, less destructive of convention than Beat. There is more respect for the accretion of human values. As an example, manners are important in Hip; the Beats say all manners are square. . . . The Beat writers seem to be getting better, more exciting. It may become a very powerful force in our literature. I think the Beat has opened the way to more excitement in our lives…."

Another statement of the Hipster philosophy comes from Ted Joans, the 31-year-old poet and one of the more interesting characters living in Greenwich Village. He says, "I'm a hipster. I'm concerned with the moral revolution in America; revolution through peace and love; we're the richest people in the world and yet we don't have truth and love. It's not what's up front that counts, it's what's in your heart and brain. There is nothing wrong with material possessions. But you should use them and not let them use you. I think everybody wants to conform, but the future of the world lies in the hands of the nonconformists…."

It's difficult for me to remember when I first ran into Mimi Margeaux. Maybe it was at a party, perhaps in a coffee shop. I might have even been formally introduced to her, as unlikely as it sounds. Mimi is 25. She is a beautiful girl, with thousands of friends, has traveled on the road frequently between her home in Chicago and San Francisco, New York, Mexico City, a thousand places. Mimi has been associated with the Beat movement for a long time. She knows all the poets, the painters and all the rest. I was walking down MacDougal Street one day when I met her and asked if she would join me in a beer at the Kettle of Fish, one of the Village's staple Beat haunts. Her conversation was characteristically candid: "There really are two kinds of Beats, people like [Kenneth] Patchen, the jazz musicians, [Norman] Mailer, Jack [Kerouac], Allen [Ginsberg], they're really Hipsters. The Beatniks are younger kids who are taking advantage of the trend. They don't know

Jerrold Heiserman (on couch), Dian Doyle (back to camera), Mimi Margeaux, Stella Pettelli (center), and San Francisco poets Philip Lamantia and Kirby Doyle (back to camera) on December 5, 1959, in musician Dave Lambert's Beat pad, 24 Cornelia Street.

what they're rebelling against. They just can't get along with their parents so they run away from home.

"I would say I'm a Hipster, but people think I'm a Beatnik.

"The longest I've held a job is about six months. In fact my whole working career is only about a year. Most of the time I've lived from saved money, unemployment, living at home, living with friends, and I was married…. I get along."

Then there's John Mitchell, who has a coffee shop called the Gaslight, right next door to the Kettle. For a couple of years the Gaslight has been sponsoring Beat poets reading from their work. Just about every poet in New York has read there at one time or another, and the shop has gained a national reputation. Recently Mitchell published an anthology of poetry called *The Gaslight Review*, which included the work of most of the poets who have read there. John is in his early thirties and is very well informed about the Beat Generation since he has lived in the Village for years and is right in the center of all the activity.

"I've been accused of being a Beatnik," he says. "Maybe it's the way I dress. Maybe I act peculiar and people become hysterical and anything that looks different to them is a Beatnik. Being Beat is really an attitude. I sympathize with these young people. I was raised during the Depression and I can have more fun with five cents than these kids can have with fifty dollars.

"With the Bomb and all, I don't blame these kids for flipping. They're rejecting the incredible mess that the adults have created in the world. Every time you pick up a newspaper you find another corrupt government official exposed. To quote Frank Lloyd Wright, this country went from barbarism to decadence without a period of culture in between. I think the Beat protest is a healthy thing.

"There is a difference between the Bohemians of twelve years ago and the Beats. Five years ago people who came here were rejecting society but they weren't raising hell; they were dejected and defeated. The old-time Bohemians were really beaten down by society. These kids haven't given up. It's a much healthier movement. The Beats aren't a formal movement, but they know what they don't want. They don't want cold wars, hot wars, military service, all the rest. One of the things they reject is a political party in a group. Some good will come from all this. It's a healthy thing and a lot of people are involved. The American people put them down because they're afraid that they don't want change and these [Beats] might change their ways. The last big thing in this country like the Beat Movement was the marches on Washington during the Depression. This movement will be stronger."

I also talked to Jack Micheline, a poet, who is associated with the Beat movement. Jack is in his early thirties and has put in his time on the road, so to speak. I'd call Jack a loner. He has a lot of friends, but he pretty much sticks to himself and his writing, which is a spontaneous, brick-and-mortar, concrete big-city type of writing.

"I want to get away from politics," Jack said. "I might have been politically active but it's all corrupt. I want to see better things happen that would help this country. I think the Beat is growing in all the arts. I've been told that the vitality of my work is identified with the Beat Generation. I'm anti-materialistic, the way I live, the way I feel, the way I think. I have no interest in becoming a millionaire. I'm interested in growing as a writer. Aside from my work I'm interested in girls.

"The Beat Generation is a way of life. All my life I've been rebelling against something or other. The reason for my rebellion is that I want to be able to be what I want, do what I want, without being restricted. I fight to remain myself. If my life means anything to me it has nothing to do with Beatniks. I've met a lot of people who weren't Beat who taught me a lot, who showed me things. A Beatnik is somebody running away from himself. Today they dress up in old clothes and hang around coffee houses. In the 1930s they joined the Communist Party. A Beatnik is the first stage of rebellion against society. Perhaps there will be an overthrow of the old order and not everything will be keyed to the machine age. You might say this is a rebellion against escalators."

The Beat Generation was practically founded in the East Harlem apartment of Mary Nichols, a 33-year-old mother of three children. Mary now lives in the Village and is a newspaper reporter and very active in politics. "I was a little girl out of Swarthmore College in those days," she says, "and I was terrified by that Go bunch, Clellon Holmes, Louis Simpson, Allen Ginsberg, all the rest. I moved to the Village to get away from all those Bohemians. Of course, they didn't have a name then. Everybody smoking pot, inviting me to wild parties, and I thought, my goodness, they are an amoral group.

"I'm not a Beatnik but I think I understand some of them. I'm really quite bourgeois myself. But if someone accused me of being bourgeois, I might say I was Beat. I don't care for labels. I suppose the way I'm living is Beat, but I'm not satisfied with it. In my wildest dreams I want to die in the St. Regis Hotel.

"It's a question of anxiety, I think, that produces the Beat Generation. It may be an anxiety for order and security, which is a funny thing to say about them, but they want a security that's more cosmic than what the average square wants. . . . Beatniks are really very political in a strange way. I think there is a relation between their rejection of politics and their concern over the H-Bomb. You can't reject something unless you're involved in it.

"I think the security the Beat person wants is knowing that he's not going to be annihilated in the next ten years. When I really think about it, I think it's possible that the human race will be destroyed in my lifetime. Perhaps that's why I always look so happy. There may be so little time, it doesn't seem worth being any other way."

Billie Holiday, 1959

The earth is older than sorrow
and the lovely flowers thereof;
man is no older than his tears,
and slavery nearly as old as love.

The first songs were of desire
or of despair in bondage,
and, surely, it was that lonely fire
or that weariness like great age
which moved the hand in the heart's night
to touch those gentle petals
and find their terrible delight.

Old as slavery and old as love
you aged in your songs beyond your tears
and bled on the secret thorn
of your terrible roses your life of years,
lost in the racial night we deny by day,
dark as the deep waters
where blind fish feed on the sea's decay.

The earth is older than sorrow,
and the grave will not betray you
as we have done and do and shall tomorrow.
O, aged beyond your songs, beyond all chains,
beyond even love, forget that subtlest human art
that changes into fear and pain
the wild, lovely flowers growing from your heart.

Robert Losada

theartist'sstudio

The Artist's Studio provided a forum for poets to read their work and meet fellow writers. It was the creative innovation of poet George Nelson Preston, whose storefront loft at 48 East 3rd Street became the "self-declared republic of New York poetry." In 1958 Preston was a sophomore at the City College of New York, where he majored in art and English. He was a member of a literary club that met in the college cafeteria until it closed. Then they headed to the East Village, where their Eastern European working-class neighbors often harassed these racially integrated young Bohemians, whose outlandish appearance and marijuana smoking provoked their ire. Blue-collar morality was further offended by the women of the group, who wore bizarre black stockings, matching their funereal all-black outfits, belying their "shockingly" loose sexual behavior.

On weekends everybody "made the scene" in Washington Square Park, where the young poets wanted to read aloud, but police at that time banned any kind of performance art in public places. Preston decided to open his studio to fellow poets, artists, and musicians, inviting them to perform. Preston invited everyone to his studio: Ted Joans, Frank O'Hara, Allen Ginsberg, Gregory Corso, Ray Bremser, Seymour Krim, Tuli Kupferberg, Meg Randall, Barbara Moraff, and Joel Oppenheimer. At the first poetry reading Preston brought out a stepladder, declaring that "poets would read from the steps of a beatific implement, not from lecterns or podiums." The Artist's Studio lasted about a year, and was the center of Beat activity in the East Village throughout 1959.

A reading, February 15, 1959, at the Artist's Studio. Jack Kerouac, arms out like a Christ figure, on ladder reading a passage from *On the Road*. Left to right: poets Ted Joans, Jose Garcia Villa, Allen Ginsberg, Edward Marshall, Gregory Corso, LeRoi Jones (now Amiri Baraka).

Kerouac, lying down during a break at the poetry reading (holding cigarette), surrounded by a circle of groupies.

Gregory Corso lights up two cigarettes during a break; Jose Garcia Villa, poet and editor of *Wake,* sits on his right.

A poetry reading on October 25, 1959. Left to right: Jud Yalkut, Ray Bremser (reading), William Morris (behind Bremser), Marc Schleifer, Bonnie Bremser (on floor), and George Nelson Preston. Preston gave a talk on the use of mescaline and peyote by American and British artists; Bremser recited "Song to a Silo."

The audience sitting comfortably on floor cushions as they listen to Stephen Levine, Robert Losada, Albert Xoc, Tuli Kupferberg, and Susan Gorbea read from their poetry, February 22, 1959.

Right page, top: Robert Losada (left), Stephen Levine (center), and Albert Xoc (right) applaud Tuli Kupferberg's reading of "Greenwich Village of My Dreams," on February 22, 1959. Levine read from his collection *A Resonance of Hope*.

Right page, bottom: Bob Lubin and Sally Stern enraptured by the sassy poetry of Ray Bremser, October 25, 1959, at The Artist's Studio.

15

C O U P L E T S

To be a spot-headed cat on a forked tree
is to be inversely what my baby is to me

I know the names of the stars from north to south
a gifted hunter with a warm song in the mouth

A february rabbit is what I hunt in may
A word in this book is closer than the sea

Women are vowels   I hear the crashing wave
' I am the queen and hope of every hive '

it could kill you

-Paul Blackburn

16

blackmountainschool

Black Mountain College, an experimental school founded in the early 1930s in Black Mountain, North Carolina, was a wellspring of avant-garde talent in the 1950s, and one of the breeding grounds of the Beat movement. The college provided backing in 1953 for the *Black Mountain Review*, under the aegis of college rector (and noted-poet) Charles Olson. Robert Creeley, a student and later an instructor, was the editor, and he provided an important outlet for those 1950s poets later known as the Black Mountain School, among them Paul Blackburn, Gilbert Sorrentino, Robert Duncan, Louis Zukofsky, Jonathan Williams, Fielding Dawson, Denise Levertov, Edward Field, Paul Goodman, and Joel Oppenheimer.

The college was a tiny community open to the most advanced ideas in the arts. In July 1952 composer John Cage put up a large tent in which he performed his avant-garde compositions. Artist Remy Charlip put programs, printed on torn pieces of toilet paper, on a table at the entrance to the tent. A bowl of tobacco stood next to the toilet paper, and the audience was invited to roll their own cigarettes. Black Mountain College brought Cage together with choreographer Merce Cunningham and painter Robert Rauschenberg, whose collaborative efforts became a model for interdisciplinary experimentation (called "Happenings" in the 1960s).

Painters Dan Rice and Jasper Johns and conceptual artist Ray Johnson were Black Mountain alumni. Rauschenberg and Johns, who studied under Franz Kline, were forerunners of Pop Art. The college closed in the spring of 1956, but its influence on the arts scene has survived its brief existence.

Poet and writer Fielding Dawson, who also contributed illustrations for the magazine, *Jargon*, and Totem Press, in the Old Colony Tap Room on Commercial Street, in Provincetown, on July 4, 1959.

Denise Levertov at the Living Theatre's reception marking Jonathan Williams's publication of two new books, November 13, 1959.

Above: Paul Blackburn in his Chelsea flat at 322 West 25th Street, September 20, 1959.

Right page: Louis Zukofsky at a cocktail party on November 12, 1962, at Lita Hornick's apartment at 888 Park Avenue. She was the chief benefactor for *Kulchur* magazine.

Above: Paul Goodman at Bruno Palmer-Poroner's Nonagon Gallery, 99 Second Avenue, on January 25, 1959.

Left page: John Wieners at an art opening for sculptor John Chamberlain and painter Alfred Leslie at the Martha Jackson Gallery, January 5, 1960.

Upside Down

Old slugger-the-bat
          don't try to control me

I've a cold in my head
and a pain in one side
          it's the cautious climate
          of birds.

Where the bitter night shows
fat as an owl the skeleton
          not counting the skin.

          This species can't bite,
but it has a hurt. We've all got birds
          flying at us

little ones over the toes.
The hand that holds is webbed
no knuckles
          but the bone grows.

Barbara Guest

thecedarstreettavern

The original Cedar Street Tavern at 24 University Place (between 8th and 9th Streets) had the distinction of not being on Cedar Street; it had no TV, no jukebox or Muzak, no skeetball. There was no attempt to enliven the decor of the bar-room. It was almost depressing in its starkness: a long bar in front, leading back to a harshly lit space with bare walls, wooden booths lined with metal studs, and small tables. The food was strictly "pub grub," with meat loaf and mashed potatoes a weekly special.

But it was *the* New York School artists' bar. In the early 1950s the bar was frequented by artists Jackson Pollock, Willem de Kooning, Franz Kline, Mark Rothko, John Chamberlain, Philip Guston, Larry Rivers, Audrey Flack, and Ruth Kligman. Dramatic tales of drunken brawls that took place at the Cedar usually featured Pollock, whose antics caused many of them. Once, in a drunken rage, he tore the bathroom door off its hinges and hurled it across the room at Franz Kline.

For the Beats, the Cedar also served as a meeting place where they could find a sympathetic ear to talk about their work, or catch up on the latest gossip. On almost any night you might see Allen Ginsberg, Jack Kerouac, Gregory Corso, Jack Micheline, Ted Joans, Diane di Prima, Joel Oppenheimer, LeRoi Jones, Paul Cummings, Tuli Kupferberg, Frank O'Hara, Hubert Selby, Jr., Paul Goodman, Julian Beck, Judith Malina, or David Amram.

The legendary Cedar Street Tavern lives on in name only, at 82 University Place, where it moved after a disastrous fire.

The original Cedar Street Tavern, October 2, 1959.

Poet Frank O'Hara (left) with New York School abstract expressionist painter Franz Kline on March 6, 1959.

LeRoi Jones and Diane di Prima, April 5, 1960, after a Living Theatre party for Seymour Krim's new book *The Beats*.

Right page, top: A view to the rear of the tavern, May 16, 1959; John Bodner was the bartender.

Right page, bottom: Hundreds of patrons flocked to the Cedar Tavern on the night of March 30, 1963 to celebrate the closing of the saloon: Jack Micheline (left) at the bar, Frank O'Hara and Barbara Guest (center), Allan Kaplan (right), and sculptor Abram Schlemowitz, in foreground.

A busy night, April 16, 1959.

Bartender John Bodner, Living Theatre founder Julian Beck, Allen Ginsberg, and poet-performance artist Dick Higgins, August 19, 1959.

Back of Town Blues

Busted drain pipes
reached high above buildings
children ran after each other
women looked out windows
with bored faces
liquor stores and saloons
did a roarin buisness
I got that back of town blues
In back alleys cars and cats
and washline rainbows
waved back and forth
Negro mothers walked fat
in a tired lazy stroll
Back of town blues
was all over faces
Store front churches
sang loud with sorrow
Gospel saviours
went to heaven
with the wretched poor
I got that back town blues
Chariots blew thier horns
for Sadie
I got that back town blues
As Cowboy Joe stood on the corner
dice rolled in the alleys
singing double six
I got that back town blues
Jimmy got drunk
on fire water an booz
Just walkin around
with
   that
      back
         of
           town
              blues

Jack Micheline

Jack Micheline

In the 1940s the art community's favorite rendezvous was at the Waldorf Cafeteria on Sixth Avenue and West 8th Street. The group that met at the Waldorf became the nucleus of The Club, which was not only a social gathering place noted for its raucous holiday parties but actually a dues-paying organization with regular Friday night discussions, film showings, poetry readings, and concerts.

The Club's list of members was a carefully guarded Who's Who of the avant-garde art world, and no outsiders were admitted to its programs unless accompanied by a bona fide dues-paying member. As the designated doorman beginning in December 1957, I was responsible for all the comings and goings each week. The history of The Club is marked by a restless series of moves: from East 8th Street to Broadway, to East 14th Street, to East 10th Street, to Second Avenue, and finally back to East 8th Street, just a few doors from its original site.

It was at The Club's New Year's Eve party on December 31, 1958, that I first photographed Jack Kerouac. On this night photographer Robert Frank brought many of the people who contributed to his film *Pull My Daisy*, a classic document of the Beat era. Both Kerouac and Ginsberg attended the party as his guests, showing how close they were to the artistic happenings of the era. Their attendance added an entirely new dimension to the proceedings, and they probably appeared as far out to the artists as they would have to the run-of-the-mill New Yorker.

Although The Club's programs encompassed a variety of subjects, those featuring members were the chief interest. There were panels on serious and not-so-serious topics, including "What We Don't Have to Do Anymore," "Patriotism in the American Home," "What's Wrong with Wrong," "Who Owns Space," and "What Is the New Academy," a theme that was debated for months.

In the early 1960s, the artists began to achieve a measure of fame. Many left the city for quieter surroundings or found work teaching at universities outside New York. Younger artists were not attracted to The Club's functions, preferring to meet in neighborhood bars. The Club disbanded in 1962.

Above: The Artist's Club New Year's party, December 31, 1958. Left to right: Writer Michael C. D. Macdonald, illustrator Nancy Ward Martin, critic Harold Rosenberg, editor Peter D. Martin, painter Franz Kline, poet Ted Joans, and artist Jimmy Cuchiara.

Right page: Jack Kerouac takes over the drums, December 31, 1958.

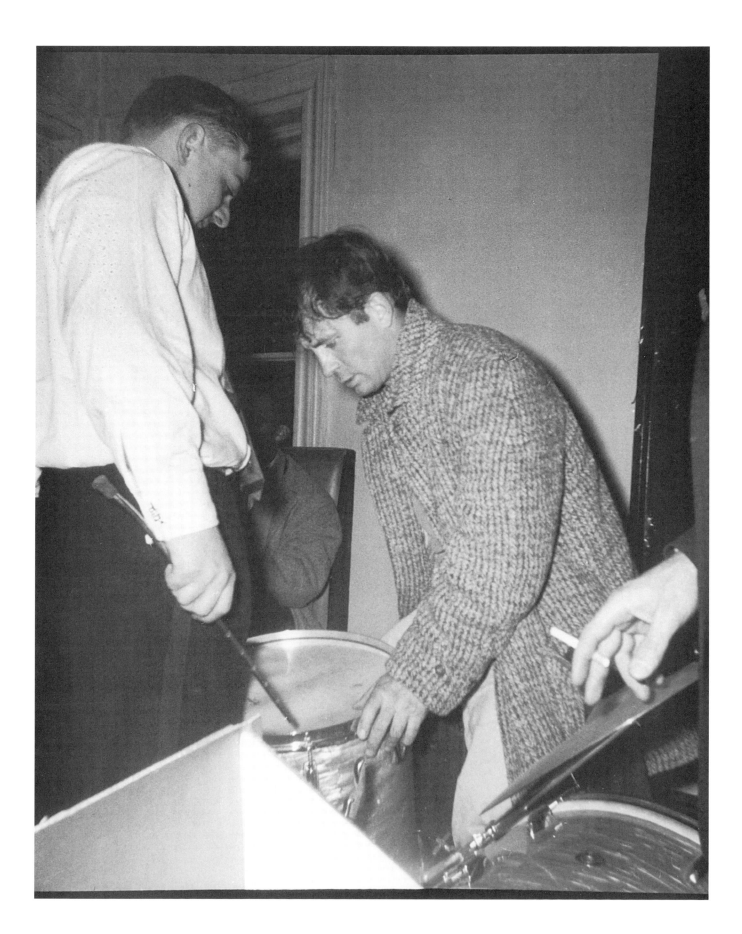

Allen Ginsberg howling at the New Year's party.

Jack Kerouac clutching a doll as he leaves the Artist's Club after the New Year's party. Next to Kerouac is his girlfriend Dody Müller (with back to the camera) and Dick Bellamy; Gregory Corso, in a white shirt, is hidden from view.

Above left: Artist Dody Müller, then Kerouac's girlfriend, at her art opening at the Hansa, an avant-garde cooperative gallery run by Dick Bellamy, on March 16, 1959.

Above right: Long-time friend of Kerouac, artist Stanley Twardowicz, with concert pianist Tamara Bliss at the Jazz Party, May 22, 1959.

Kerouac with photographer-filmmaker Robert Frank at Dody Müller's show. Frank brought the entire cast of *Pull My Daisy* to the Artist's Club's 1958 New Year's party. Jimmy Cuchiara is in the background.

Left to right: Paddy Chayefsky, Seymour Krim, and Ted Joans at The Club's Jazz Party, May 22, 1959.

A panel discussion at The Club, then located at 73 Fourth Avenue, on February 13, 1959, entitled "A Little Room for Feeling, Symbolism, and Meaning in Abstract Art." Left to right: Daniel Schneider, Allen Ginsberg, Hubert Crehan (moderator), Sonia Gechtoff, Peter Selz, and John Ferren.

A poetry reading on March 11, 1960. Left to right: Gilbert Sorrentino (standing), Diane di Prima, Max Finstein, LeRoi Jones, Joel Oppenheimer. The Club was then holding its meetings in Edith Stephen's dance studio at 144 Second Avenue.

Left to right: Lucia Dlugoszewski and Joseph LeSueur (seated); Frank O'Hara, Mike Kanemitsu, and Ronald Bladen (standing); and Golda Lewis (seated, foreground) listening to a Club panel discussion on "What Is the New Academy?, Part II," on March 20, 1959.

NOCTURNE

the highbridge body, roach, walks
on thin legs
limps slightly; dreamsweat makes acid
my pajamas; the sheet moves
with your breathing

light
dapples the ceiling, undermines the
walls; (cars pass); the child
stirs, but she does not cry;
wind climbs the fire-escape and shakes the window
    knees
    rise
    and
    fall

in this new york, cell on monastic
cell, they sleep, we sleep; dreams
stream from the women's hair;
the highbridge roach
walks
where the kitchen was;
ice claws the windows, wind
unlocks the door

how many nights shall I lie at your side
wearing pajamas; using a separate
pillow

coffeehouses

European-style coffee house—where for the price of a cup of espresso you could hang out for hours, read, or play chess—were unknown in New York City, outside of Greenwich Village and Little Italy, in the late 1940s and 1950s. And only in the Village coffee houses, on MacDougal Street and West 3rd and Bleecker Streets, did Beat writers and poets come to read poetry. Some of the cafes charged a nominal admission charge of twenty-five cents to help support the programs once they became popular.

Early coffee houses included David's, which opened in the late 1940s at 99 MacDougal; the Figaro, 186 Bleecker; and the Rienzi, 107 MacDougal. Their success led the way for an astonishing number of new places, some situated side-by-side. On West 3rd Street, the Bizarre, the Epitome, and the Caravan cafes flourished along with strip joints. The most popular readings of Beat Generation poetry were at the Gaslight, downstairs at 116 MacDougal, and at the Bizarre and Epitome.

The coffee house programs attracted not only young intellectuals, but also the anger of local nightspots that considered poetry readings unfair competition, by offering live "entertainment." Nightclub owners wanted the police to close down the coffee houses, or else force them to pay for cabaret licenses, an expensive proposition for a small business. Naturally, the coffee houses objected to this demand, and eventually the nightclub owners relented.

When the city finally ruled that coffee houses could provide "entertainment" without a cabaret license, it seemed that poetry readings were assured continued existence. But as the Beat writers dispersed, folk and chamber music concerts replaced readings. Pantomime acts, sex lectures, political discussions, and short plays drew audiences in the 1960s.

Ted Joans and fellow poets at the Gaslight Cafe, July 12, 1959. Seated left to right: L. S. M. Kelly, Joan Block, and Barbara Moraff. An ice cream soda was the drink of choice because the poetry cafes didn't serve liquor.

Editor-writer Yaakov Kohn of the *East Village Other* and Gaslight Cafe proprietor John Mitchell in front of the cafe, 116 MacDougal Street, May 15, 1960, being interviewed for a Mike Wallace special on the Beat Generation.

Listening to Beat poetry by Ted Joans, William Morris, and Hugh Romney in the Cafe Bizarre, 106 West 3rd Street, June 7, 1959.

Ted Joans in front of his self-portrait announcing a poetry reading at the Cafe Bizarre, 106 West 3rd Street, August 25, 1959.

Above: The atmosphere and decor were reminiscent of the Arabian Nights in the Caravan Cafe. Ann Winter, artist and United Nations translator (wearing eyepatch), was a member of the Artist's Club.

Left page: William Morris reading poetry at the Caravan Cafe, 102 West 3rd Street, May 24, 1959. Stage props included lit candles and plastic palm trees and daisies. Morris's love poem, "Return to New York," began: "I want to score for love my sweet; I want to hear once more the bedspring music of your kiss...."

Caravan Club manager Frank LoPiccolo being issued a summons by Sixth Precinct Officer George Parker on May 24, 1959, for conducting poetry readings without a cabaret license.

Rick Allmen's Cafe Bizarre, 106 West 3rd Street, June 7, 1959. Painter Larry Rivers had a studio upstairs. The entire block was torn down in December 1983 to make way for a New York University law-school dormitory.

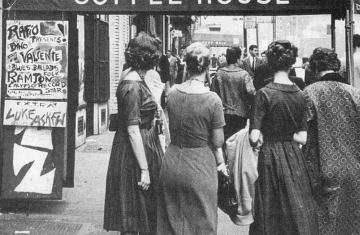

Above: The Commons Cafe had two entrances, one at 13 Minetta Street and the other at 105 MacDougal Street. It was one of the few cafes that featured neither music, poetry, nor theater; it was considered a chess player's hangout.

Left: Cafe Rafio, 165 Bleecker Street, October 16, 1960. The cafe's manager, Ronald Von Ehmsen, was shot three times and killed with a 32-calibre revolver on March 30, 1963, in front of the cafe by a 73-year-old tenant in the building who faced eviction so that the coffee house could be enlarged.

Hugh Romney, in a linen suit and Brooks Brothers tie, reading poetry, on June 12, 1959. In the *Gaslight Poetry Review*, Romney's poem, "Let the Last Be First," an ode to love, began: "Wings beat noisily! Golden harps rejoice! Angels copulate...." Romney was the best-dressed Beatnik in Greenwich Village, but all that changed years later when he transformed himself into Wavy Gravy, famous for his work as announcer at the first Woodstock festival.

Richard Davidson reading his poem "Moon Over MacDougal Street," at the Epitome Cafe, July 19, 1959.

Ray Bremser, on June 6, 1959, reading "Poem of Holy Madness," at the Epitome Cafe.

Diane di Prima, on June 18, 1959, reading from her first published book of poetry, *This Kind of Bird Flies Backward.*

Jazz poet Jim Lyons (left) with Malcolm Soule, on September 21, 1959, at the Gaslight Cafe.

Rick Allmen of Café Bizarre and John Mitchell of Gaslight Café at 8th Street and Sixth Avenue, June 26, 1960.

I Beg You Come Back & Be Cheerful

Tonite I got hi in the window of my apartment
          chair at 3: AM
gazing at Blue incandescent torches
          bright-lit street below
clotted shadows looming on a new laid pave
--as last week Medaeval rabble
          plodded thru the brown raw
          dirt turned over
                    ...

and tired ladies sitting
          garbage pails
                    ...

          the Fire Hydrant
the sun at 5 P.M. throwing ...
now all dark outside, a cat
          the street silent
and she looks up, and passerby ...
          pile of rubble
to a golden shining ...
          (phosphor in the dark
                    ...

          (as ...
--Thinking America ...
Police clog the streets ...
Prowl cars creak & ...

Today a woman, 20, slapped ...
          playing with her ...
Saying with a sad ...
          "Don't do that ..."
And there was no ...
          I looked around ...
a pile of crap in the ...

          Your goal Dynamite! Mustache!
I'll grow a beard and carry lovely
          bombs,
I will destroy the world, stip in between
          the cracks of Death
And change the Universe—ha!
I have the secret, I have
          Universes naked in
                    my ...
"Garlic, Poverty, a will to ...,
          a strange dream in my meat!

Thanks to the success of his poem "Howl," Allen Ginsberg became a spokesman for the fledgling Beat movement, as well as one of its most notorious figures. He was one of the first Village figures to emerge on the national scene, and as such could draw audiences anywhere in New York.

Ginsberg changed the voice of American poetry and became a central figure in the counterculture. In his early years at Columbia University, he was suspended twice, once for writing "Butler has no balls" (referring to university president Nicholas Murray Butler) on the window of his dormitory room and for letting Kerouac sleep overnight in his room; another time for getting involved in a robbery after he stored stolen goods in his room for Herbert Huncke, a small-time junkie who was a friend of Ginsberg's and William Burroughs's.

At Columbia, Ginsberg met Kerouac, Burroughs, and Lucien Carr. Kerouac and Carr had already formulated a literary New Vision, which "held truthful self-expression of one's own experience—one's own mind—to be paramount." Ginsberg moved to San Francisco in 1954, where he met Peter

allenginsberg:beat-at-large

Orlovsky. In 1955, Ginsberg's famous first reading of "Howl" at San Francisco's Six Gallery, and the ensuing trial for obscenity after the poem was published by City Lights Books, marked the onslaught of media interest in Ginsberg and the Beat movement.

Ginsberg and Orlovsky moved to 170 East 2nd Street, on Manhattan's Lower East Side, in August 1958, to an apartment with four medium-sized rooms, steam heat, hot water, shower, and refrigerator; the rent was $60. There Ginsberg wrote "Kaddish," personalizing the traditional Jewish memorial prayer for the dead in memory of his mother, who died in Pilgrim State Hospital on Long Island. The poem was published by City Lights Books in 1961; the first line reads: "Strange now to think of you, gone without corsets & eyes, while I walk on the sunny pavement of Greenwich Village." After twenty nonstop hours Ginsberg had written fifty-eight pages. I was fortunate to be able to photograph Ginsberg at home, to reveal another, less flamboyant side of his personality.

On February 5, 1959, Ginsberg returned in triumph (although not without controversy) to give a reading at Columbia University's McMillin Theatre. Ginsberg, accompanied by Gregory Corso and Peter Orlovsky, brought a crowd of 1,400 people into the hall, with some 500 more outside,

unable to gain entrance. Kerouac was also scheduled to read but never showed up. Professor Frederick W. Dupee, who taught the college's course on modern British and American poetry and was literary editor of the socialist newspaper *The New Masses* and a founder of the *Partisan Review*, introduced the poets.

To the audience of students and a few faculty members, Orlovsky and Corso were unknown quantities, their work puzzling. Ginsberg, though, made a powerful impression, reading from his new poem, "Kaddish," which impressed his listeners with the immediacy of his grief and the intensity of his delivery.

This reading at Columbia has assumed a mythic importance in the history of the Beats. Ginsberg's persona as a twentieth-century Whitman, a visionary poet who used everyday language, was validated and would eventually reach out to mainstream America, where recognition of his work would far exceed the usual limited audience for poetry.

                    I Beg You Come Back & Be Cheerful

Tonite I got hi in the window of my apartment
            chair at 3: AM
gazing at Blue incandescent torches
            bright-lit street below
clotted shadows looming on a new laid pave
--as last week Medaeval rabbis
            plodded thru the brown raw
            dirt turned over--sticks
                & cans
    and tired ladies sitting on spanish
            garbage pails--in the deadly heat
                    --one month ago
            the fire hydrants were awash--
    the sun at 3 P.M, today in a haze--
now all dark outside, a cat crosses
            the street silently--I meow
and she looks up, and passes a
            pile of rubble on the way
    to a golden shining garbage pail
            (phosphor in the night
                    & alley stink)
        (or door-can mash)
        --Thinking America is a chaos
Police clog the streets with their anxiety,
    Prowl cars creak & halt!

Today a woman, 20, slapped her brother
            playing with his infant bricks--
    toying with a huge rock--
            "Don't do that now! the cops! the cops!"
And there was no cop there--
            I looked around my shoulder--
    a pile of crap in the opposite direction.

            Tear gas! Dynamite! Mustaches!
I'll grow a beard and carry lovely
        bombs,
I will destroy the world, slip in between
            the cracks of death
    And change the Universe--Ha!
I have the secret, I carry
            Subversive salami in
                    my ragged briefcase
    "Garlic, Poverty, a will to Heaven,"
        a strange dream in my meat!

(Clouds ~~and~~ Radiance[T]), I have heard God's voice in
          my sleep, or Blake's awake, or my own or
the dream of a delicatessen of snorting cows
          and bellowing pigs--
               The chop of a knife
          a finger severed in my brain--
               a few deaths I know--

          O brothers of the Laurel
Is the world real?
               Is the Laurel
a joke or a crown of thorns?--

               Fast, pass
               up the ass
               Down I go
               Cometh Woe

--the street outside,
          me spying on New York.
The dark truck passes snarling &
          vibrating deep--

What
     if
        the
            worlds
            were
            a
              series
                    of steps

                         What
                         if
                         the
                         steps
                    joined
               back
               at
          the
Margin

Leaving us flying like birds into Time
          --the eyes and car headlights--
          or senses--The shrinkage of emptiness
in the Nebulae

These Galaxies cross like pinwheels & they pass
               like gas--
What forests are born.

                         Allen Ginsberg
                         September 15, 1959

                         (unpublished)

Above: Professor Frederick W. Dupee of the Columbia University English Department introduces Peter Orlovsky, Gregory Corso, and Allen Ginsberg.

Right page: Gregory Corso reads from his poem "Marriage," described as "a compulsive poem about a compulsive subject."

Allen Ginsberg reads several poems, including "Kaddish," "The Ignu," and "Lion in the Room," which he dedicated to Lionel Trilling, his former professor.

Peter Orlovsky's contributions to the evening were two wacky poems. "Lines of Feeling" started with "The mountain bear has a hole in his pants—trouble...."

Reassembled at Columbia some sixteen years after the famous reading, on April 17, 1975, Gregory Corso, William Burroughs, Allen Ginsberg, and Peter Orlovsky (left to right) celebrated by giving a new reading. (Burroughs, of course, was not at the original event.)

Allen Ginsberg's tenement flat at 170 East 2nd Street, January 9, 1960. Lafcadio (left), and Peter Orlovsky, and Allen Ginsberg.

Ginsberg's refrigerator, with a picture of Edgar Allan Poe on the left, Charles Baudelaire on the right.

Ginsberg removes his glasses and eyeballs the camera.

Above: With his Siamese cat.

Right page: At the typewriter.

Herbert Huncke (left) and Peter Orlovsky.

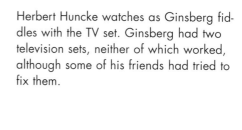

Herbert Huncke watches as Ginsberg fiddles with the TV set. Ginsberg had two television sets, neither of which worked, although some of his friends had tried to fix them.

Ginsberg's apartment overlooked an all-night Jewish bakery. Noisy trucks went back and forth all night long. The bakery had a big clock in the window, which was helpful to Ginsberg who didn't own a clock.

Ginsberg in bed; a dagger-like cross on the wall is lodged between the wall sconces.

The kitchen sink.

RHYTHM

up   where the eve n ing light is
spee da/   ah shoo/ day spa/ doo

shift ing soft and   low is rhythm
ah/   sha da/ sha da spoo dee/ah sha yah da

up where bodies clasp with
ah sha/ spa doo/ah/   sha

meters soul is rhythm
doo   ah/   bla blew swee dee /

senses swing   images bring
spwee bwee dee/spa ya da/

desired things sublime
spur   spa   spwee shoo ah yah/

flesh plays melodically upon
sha   yah   da/sha da / yah dah/

the flesh of rhythms mind
spee swoo sha dee ooh ah

up where the   evening light
spee da/   spa shoo/sha   dah/

now dims with   secret glow
spa shoo/ya dee/ah   swee/

is   rhythm
shoop sha swoop swee/

up where hearts sound in the dark
spa dee spa/ swee   ah da /

for love is the rhythm
ah sha sha ba da ba /

of the soul
sha ah ba swee ah /

jazzandthebeats

Reading poetry to jazz was a San Francisco phenomenon that poets like Kenneth Rexroth and Kenneth Patchen started in the mid-1950s. The first jazz and poetry event in Greenwich Village was at the Brata Gallery, 89 East 10th Street, on November 19, 1957, when Jack Kerouac, Philip Lamantia, and Howard Hart, a jazz drummer as well as a poet, read poetry to the music of David Amram's French horn. That event was followed by a week-long engagement, starting on December 19, 1957, with Kerouac and Steve Allen at the Village Vanguard, 178 Seventh Avenue South. The audience was not sympathetic. As Kerouac read a piece called "The Life of a Sixty Year Old Mexican Junkie," some people snickered, others ignored him. It is ironic that many years later Kerouac's readings with Steve Allen's music became the inspiration and source for a boxed album issued by Rhino Records.

Although there were occasional poetry and jazz events at the Living Theatre, the combination moved on to the jazz clubs, which remained popular with Beat writers and the downtown art community. The Jazz Gallery, 80 St. Marks Place, featured the Horace Silver quintet with Art Farmer and Benny Golsson, and Art Blakey and his Jazz Messengers. At the Five Spot, 2 St. Marks Place, the walls were plastered with announcements of art openings, poetry readings, and jazz concerts. The regulars included John Coltrane, Thelonious Monk, Ornette Coleman, Cecil Taylor, and Charlie Mingus. Artists Larry Rivers on the saxophone and Howard Kanovitz at the piano were impromptu performers.

The Beats's interest in jazz helped spread the music beyond the small community of jazz lovers. The Beats appropriated the language of the "hip" jazzster, and often wrote poems in blues or jazz-influenced formats. Kerouac and other Beat writers liked to think of themselves as "improvising" at the typewriter just as a jazz musician might with his or her instrument. Just as Beat literature was treated as decidedly lower-class, most critics at the time looked down their noses at jazz music as distinctly second-rate; the Beats were among the first "serious" writers to elevate the musicians to the legendary status they deserved.

Charles Mingus at the Five Spot Cafe, August 22, 1962. Mingus's group played there regularly, and poets frequently read their works to his jazz arrangements.

An afternoon of poetry and jazz at the Five Spot Cafe, February 22, 1964, brought together Ginsberg (left), Corso (right), Joel Oppenheimer (in doorway), LeRoi Jones, Hubert Selby, Jr., and Gilbert Sorrentino for the benefit of Present Stages, an East Village theater group. Posters on the far right wall advertise shows at many art galleries.

Art Blakey and his Jazz Messengers at the Jazz Gallery, February 6, 1960.

Seated at the rear table, left to right, Zadie Parkinson, Alfred Leslie, and Harold (Doc) Humes at the Jazz Gallery, December 15, 1959. The Horace Silver Quintet, Art Farmer, and Benny Golsson played that night. The painting on the wall is by Al Leslie and is hung sideways. The title of the work is "Kurtz's Station," from the Joseph Conrad novel *Heart of Darkness*.

Holiday magazine staged a "Beatnik party" for a photo feature on May 24, 1959, held in painter Maurice Bugeaud's waterfront loft. And what would a true Beat party be without a jazz band? Left to right: Walter Bowe, Ahmad Abdul-Malik, Ken Davern, Ephram Resnick, Danny Barker (behind Bowe, barely visible).

Betsy Zogbaum (seated, left), Franz Kline, Larry Rivers (standing), Howard Kanovitz, Joyce Johnson, and (in foreground) Cynthia Fancher, at the Jazz Gallery, April 24, 1960, at an after-theater party.

Larry Rivers playing jazz saxophone with Howard Kanovitz at the piano, April 24, 1960, at the Jazz Gallery.

Bass player Charles Mingus and San Francisco poet Kenneth Patchen perform together at the Living Theatre, March 16, 1959.

and throw shovels into
Lets play something
Lets play something dar
lets all go to Central P
and strip...then piss o
Lets play something

lets play that we are m

lets stop playing with
in the pants because he
tall dark and handsome
Let's play something
Lets play that we are
lets reflect the worl
lets be chips off the c
Lets play something
Lets play something
Like standing around
solved stoned li

90

Lets play something

tedjoans's birthdayparty

Ted Joans was born on the Fourth of July on a riverboat docked in Cairo, Illinois. He grew up on the riverboat, where his father was an entertainer. When he was 12, his father gave him a trumpet, but Joans had other ambitions. After studying for a fine arts degree, he went to New York to become a painter.

He soon met Gregory Corso, Allen Ginsberg, and Peter Orlovsky. Ginsberg persuaded Joans to write poetry, and his friend Langston Hughes encouraged Joans to read his poems like a jazz soloist. Joans made poetry entertaining, and he gained a following in the United States, Europe, and Africa.

As part of my Rent-A-Beatnik scheme in the late 1950s, Joans took his message to the 'burbs in Scarsdale and Tuxedo Park. He preached his "Sermon" to an audience

that had paid to hear him read lines like, "Get rid of the umbilical cord that your Dragass prejudiced parents have around your neck." His mission as ambassador for the Beat Generation was to create public acceptance for poetry as one of the livelier arts.

Joans's birthday parties were legendary. Everyone was welcome; there was no such thing as a list of invited guests. Attendance mushroomed to a group of staggering size, usually including artists, writers, poets, critics, and barflies looking for free booze; some guests brought their own bottles, which disappeared quickly. I was able to document one of these legendary parties on the evening of Saturday, July 25, 1959, when the usual group of Village denizens gathered for a wild celebration.

Playmates future Laymates

Let's play something
lets get togather
and then stuff them into the TV tubes with the commericals
our parents that is
Lets play something
lets drive around town and sling white paint at happylooking people
and throw shovels into spade store front church windows
Lets play something
Lets play something daring
lets all go to Central Park at midnight
and strip...then piss on everyone that we encounter
Lets play something

  lets play that we are no longer kids

  lets stop playing with Gino cause he is an Italian and kick Hymie
  in the pants because he's Jewish and forbid our sisters from dating
  tall dark and handsome Dinky cause he's Negro
  Let's play something
Llets play that we are all mirrors
  lets reflect the world that we live in
lets be chips off the old square blocks
    Lets play something
    Lets play something silly
    Like standing around at the base of a statue and try to drink our
             selved stoned like the statue

  Lets play something
  lets play something sexy..like getting into bed..even adding overcoat
  and gloves...and then try to copulate through all that clothing and
  give a prize to the first one that has a climax with out physical @
                                                      contact

   Lets Play Something
Lets Play something horrible...############,You be Hitler
  and you be Mussilini,and you be Stalin,and you be Tojo, and you
  be Strijdom of South Africa and I'll be Gov.Faubus
Wow what a cast of devils ..Yeah lets play that
###Lets play something,Lets play anything
  Lets play bohemian ...and wear odd clothes....and grew a beard or a
  poneytail..live in the Village for 200.00 a month for one small pad
  and stroll through Washington Square Park with guitarslooking sad
Lets play something
   Lets play that we are all adult westerns..and we have for big lying
   sponsers on TV..and lets dont use our guns or horses
   But use psychology and ride women at night on the indoor prarie
   Lets Play something
   Lets play that we are all Ivy Leaguers
   with belts in the back of all articles of clothing including our socks
   and ties..Lets look toward Wall Street and Madison Avenue for a @
   future..and lets believe some cigar smoking pot belly when he offers
   us a life time job with his firm..but lets not forget there are H-bombs
   to make this so-called 'lifetime job' a damn lie
   Lets play that we are all creeps
   Lets play that we hang out with the 42nd st preverts
   and sit in the smelly movies all daylong and urinate under the seats
   and feel the legs of unwary movies goers
   Lets Play something

Lets play that we are all SAFE
    lets play that we all work from 9 til 5
     and we are trying to pay for that split level home in Westchester
with built in wife and two kids,and the inevitable wall to wall carpets
and trying to keep up the never ending payments on the flashy car,color
   TV,hi-fi,wash n dry,deep freeze, doctor bills and the other keeping
     up with the Jones deals
    Lets play something
Lets play that we are all gay
    and we have invested our selves in a fruity career
 and be sincere and switch our homosexual tails up and down West 8th st
    And sit on the Washington Square meat rack and pounce upon some rich
    square and rape him on a fire hydrant
Lets play something
Lets play that we are all Russians, living in Russia to day
    Lets play that we are really, the squarest of the squares in the world
     Lets live behind our communist curtain,and force our way our life on
 others, and then with a threatning hammer and sickle call them brothers
   Lets outlaw jazz,beautiful slinky chicks, and creative arts
  Lets play something
    Lets Play that we are all policemen and be called the fuzz
    Lets play that we are all politicans and be called crooked
    Lets play that we are all balletdancers and be called queers
    Lets play that we are all poets and artists and be called crazy
    Lets play that we are all Square Conventional Spoiled American females
 and believe what the TV commericals say..& read the Sat.Eve Post
 and Ladies Home Journal .and at night dream of rape all day talk too
much, & till the end of time work our men to death trying to keep up
with the Jones,lets also wear too much cosmetics,call men cute, and
 continue to rule 3/4 of America the north east west,and be the best
    in bed undressed
    Lets Play something
     Lets play anything
    Lets play that we are aall the poor sad animals locked in the cages
in the zoos..and lets play that we dream about our former homelands
and lets play that we plan to escape at midnight New Year eve night
and mingle with the crowd at Times Square that night before leaving
   Lets Play Something Lets Play Anything
   Lets play that we are all hipsters..and be spiritually involved with life
 and dig all things creative ..and ball a whole lots..and be happy in
 poetry and art..and travel all allover the world,digging everything,
  loving every swinging soul,picking up on all jazz, experiencing all
    great kicks,be chicks & cats avoiding conformity,confessing the truth,
 disafilated from the goof,digging freedom, and wail cool before the world
Yeah ladies and gentlemen
 lets play that
    Lets play that we are all hipsters and really begin to LIVE

                        by ted joans
                        March 1958
                        revision Sept 59

to fredmcdarrah
     from
    tedjoans
Sept 15, 59 NYC

Attention Girls of the Beat Generation

Call AI 4-0796 for address or eat at the Gaslight And find out

Art Sex Food

One must wait before the cop out now be fore you loose your mind be cool and be happy

The Jazz Sermon Jazz dig baby Goose Jazz swing forth with me and your

So you want to be hip little girl

There it is - yep - thats it hip chic...

you must you should you shall you...

like I dig baby Goose

I love you as I Ke love Jazz

He that slippeth is a goofer

Like man the fuzz busted a cat in his pad for he was a doulik

Bring your mother till told that's a tony

Hip Happy Hip Hip Hip

The Sermon I want you to find your even by doing

Best Poetry

Sat nite July 25 at 10:0'clock til 10:0'clock sun morn you are invited to ted Joans birthday Party bit So be present with a present and bring other Chicklets-chicks-and even hip hens. only cats with written invitations will be admitted. But girls free

Top: Sculptor Jackie Ferrara (left, in gingham dress), earthworks artist Bob Smithson (rear, in striped sport shirt), filmmaker Robert Frank (center, in white shirt and tie).

Bottom: Artists and poets dancing at Joans's Beatnik birthday party. Filmmaker Kenneth Van Sickle (rear left, in striped shirt), Robert Beauchamp (center, in white dress shirt), and Jackie Ferrara (in gingham dress, center).

Left page: Party announcement poster is specifically addressed to young "chicks" and "chicklets"; also emphasizes the three words "art; sex; food" above Joans's raised fingers.

95

Ted Joans, wearing a black cowboy hat and striped shirt, presides over the mayhem. Dan List (in straw hat), earthworks artist Bob Smithson behind List, and painter Gene Kates dancing in center.

Top: Poet John Brent (left), painter and manager of the Epitome Coffee Shop, painter Larry Poons, and Joe Bolero (with toilet seat around his neck).

Bottom: Ballentine ale, Schlitz beer, and gallon jugs of Italian wine were very popular; artist Larry Poons (far right).

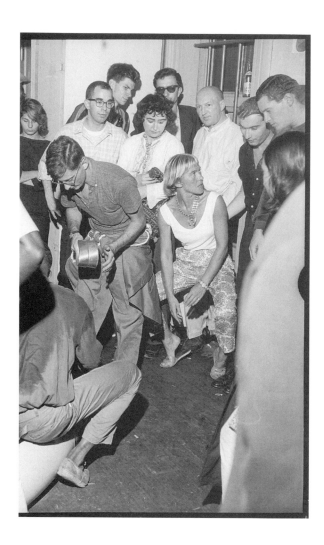 

Above left: Bongo drums and aluminum pots make music. Bob Smithson at rear center.

Above right: Bob Lubin and Steve Mildwoff, a nephew of Louise Nevelson.

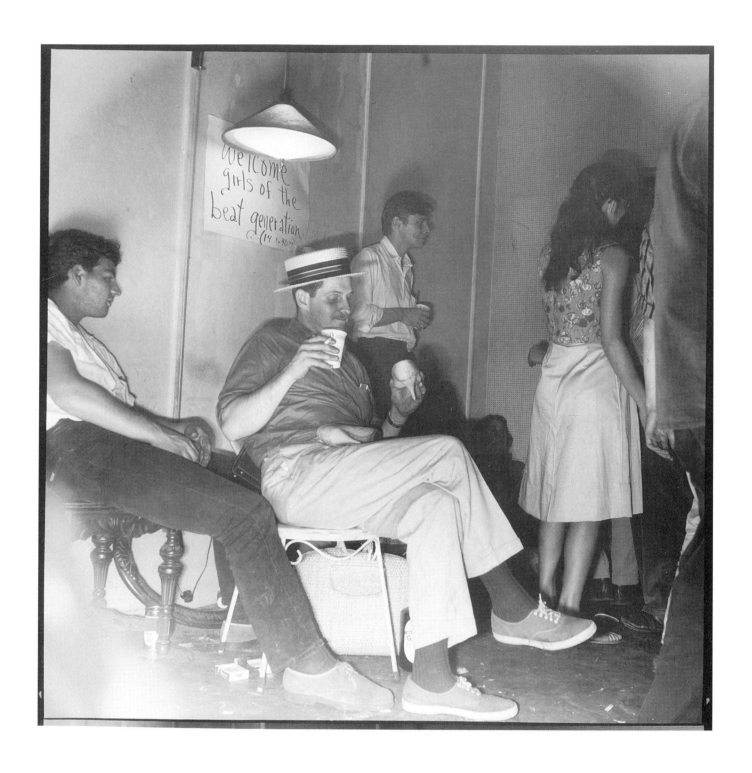

Village Voice auto columnist Dan List inspects a shoe; filmmaker Frank Simon in background. The sign on the wall welcomes girls of the Beat Generation, ages 14 to 40.

Party guests sit on the floor under graffiti, "The Blood of the Poets," scrawled on the wall by Nicoli Welsh.

The mattress was convenient for catnaps between cans of beer.

In the boat" - Basho

Whiter than the roc
~~Thisxxautumnxwind~~ ~~white~~
This Autumn wind ----BA

Shiro yama no
Ishi yori shiroshi
Aki no kase ----BASH

Hail to Harold Goldfinge

Jack K

kerouac writes a poem

Kerouac compiled a list of thirty precepts for writing that appeared in his "Belief and Technique for Modern Prose," published in *Evergreen Review* in 1959. His List of Essentials included: "Write what you want bottomless from bottom of the mind; Remove literary, grammatical and syntactical inhibition; Write in recollection and amazement for yourself; Composing wild, undisciplined, pure coming in from under, crazier the better; You're a Genius all the time."

He certainly followed those precepts on December 10, 1959, the evening he and two friends from San Francisco, Albert Saijo and Lew Welch, visited our West 14th Street apartment to compose a poem for my photo/poetry anthology *The Beat Scene*. The three of them had recently driven east in Welch's Jeep. The session began quietly, as we sipped drinks. We then showed Jack photos taken the previous New Year's Eve. As the whiskey, gin, and beer disappeared, each of them contributed a line of poetry, in turn, as Gloria took it down on an old Underwood typewriter.

By 11 P.M., the poem, a series of haikus based on their cross-country trip, was finished. He read it aloud for final approval. We then headed for the Egyptian Gardens to watch belly dancers and have a few drinks. Then we picked up a reluctant Allen Ginsberg still in his pajamas and went to Chinatown for a late dinner at the Golden Dragon. After that, Kerouac, Gloria, and I went to the Five Spot to hear Ornette Coleman; the place was nearly empty except for Franz Kline and William Morris. Last stop was a loft on Chambers Street, where we all smoked pot until 5 A.M.

this is what its called —

THIS IS A POEM BY ALBERT SAIJO? LEW WELCH AND JACK KEROUAC

At the second coming I want my navy knit cap

(Worn inside out)

I insist on my survival diaphragm, what am I a girl

No more immaculate conceptions

Oh, let's get really poetic

Big white space

The lorn are rude to the turning shoe

Which is literally true they have one in Lost Davis

Angel ma

\# In Lost Davis there is a motel called the Blue Angel with an 18 foot

blue angel with big tits spinning in the winter desert air

Hippotamouses are gigantic river pigs

Grain elevators are giant trucks waiting for the road to approach them

~~Whereresendx~~

East St. Louis: whore candy

\# I'd like to sleep in Joplin in little catches

It began to snow lightly in southern Illinois

There were rabbit tracks in motel driveways

The interminable potato cooker gossiped

~~Anoxthaxkxdixxxxxkdxtkxrxx~~
JK: ~~asks~~
~~Waxxxxxx~~ the Indian what's the local saying around here
~~Indian!~~ He ~~said~~ there are none around here

    I pledge to my customers as a Texaco dealer
    that my registered bathroom shall remain fully
    equipped and clean.

Isn't that sick?

Thexxxxxxx

Thou irk'st but for gain

Gloria you arent getting the punctation

\# I saw a white horse standing

In an abandoned store front

\# I knew the mistery of the east

I heard that dog barking behind the mangy door

He was guarding the door nobody wanted

The last time I was in Amarillo

I smoked my first cigar

And Roosevelt died.

In log cabin motel

New Lincolns

Dream Van Doren.

I truned into a gas station

The engine stopped.

In safeway parking lots

Old men drive slowly

Backwards.

Lewisxxxxxxxxxxxxxx

kneelx
itxxxxxthexexxxxxxxxx
andxxxxxxxxxxxxxxxxx
inxArizonax

                                        high
In Arizona they put a cross beisde the driveway wherever somebody was
killed. Large cross for adults, small cross for children. Seeing
these we said let's stop and steal one. It was sunset. Purple cowboys
with mouths of dust were ranging far for the heifer of the lord.
Ran out of the car, saw the tip of the cross against the Arizona sunset
and said I have to see it. Knelt. Forced to kneel. Found myself
kneeling in thorns.

In Texas
Leo's cock
Turned to glass.
And he wrapped it in gold foil.

Driving across the U.S.A. 75 miles an hour
Leo with his cock of port
Passing trains

When milady dreams
I dream of thinking

When milady unbuckles her pursey eye
I bcount her shoe tongues1
And dream of 14 year old Puerto Rican girls
with Balthus eyes

Villon yslipped tresors into his boys

On a disappearing road,
Among crenelated mountains
Thinking about whores, that girl in Chicago in a tub   oysters — *italo*

We left the civilized plains of the middle west
for the mountain canyons, flora fauna of New York

Everyone goes home alone
Under the 2,000 foot ceiling of Manhattan

"Spring evening -
The sound of the frog
Jumping in the pond" - Basho

"Midday sun -
The mad girl singing
In the boat" - Basho

Whiter than the ~~stone~~ rocks of ~~mountain~~ *white mountain*
~~Thisxxxxwhitexxxxxxwhite mountain,~~
This Autumn wind   ----BASHO

Shiro yama ~~x~~ no
Ishi yori shiroshi
Aki no kase   ----BASHO

Hail to Harold Goldfinger

Jack Kerouac   Lew Welch   Albert Saijo

Jack Kerouac, Gloria Schoffel, Lew Welch, and Albert Saijo writing a poem at Fred and Gloria's apartment, 304 West 14th Street, December 10, 1959.

Kerouac begins the first line: "At the Second Coming I want my Navy knit cap (Worn inside out)."

Lew Welch in a jolly mood contributes two haikus: "Oh, let's get really Poetic. Big White Space." Saijo sits quietly waiting his turn.

Kerouac uses index finger to tap the keys as Gloria Schoffel waits for the next line. Whiskey bottles on the coffee table help the lines flow smoothly.

Kerouac tackles the Underwood with, "I know the misery of the East/I heard that dog barking behind the mangy door/He was guarding the door nobody wanted."

Kerouac shouts out for Saijo to type in his contribution.

Albert Saijo pounds out the last haiku: "Shiro Yama no Ishi yori shiroshi Aki no nase-Busho/Hail to Harold Goldfinger!"

Kerouac reads over the finished poem, which was first published in *The Beat Scene*. A longer version by the three men appeared in 1973 as "Trip Trap, Haiku Along the Road from San Francisco to New York 1959."

Kerouac declares it's time to relax, now that the poem is finished along with all the beer and whiskey. An original and one carbon copy of the poem was made and titled "This a poem by Albert Saijo, Lew Welch and Jack Kerouac."

Everyone was pleased with the final version. Kerouac smoked his last cigarette and suggested going to the Egyptian Gardens, his favorite nightclub, which featured belly dancers.

A nightclub photographer took this photo in the Egyptian Gardens, 301 West 29th Street, of Albert Saijo, Gloria Schoffel, Jack Kerouac, Lew Welch, and Fred McDarrah celebrating the finished haiku poem. A Chinese dinner and some pot smoking completed the evening.

OPEN LETTER TO LIFE MAGAZINE

Sickle moon terror nails replica in tin ginsberg. Replicas of Squaresville — grey piebald pigeons — pointedly questioned, mimic each other. The wet concrete square — a boy wit police — is ate by literat birds. Pitiful personal lives of suspension, flapping frantic, come to stare. An opium eater and Vincent-visitors bathe their feet in San Francisco market-deal of the world's art-compacted-feathers. Sunbrow those third street bums on se. Some kind a fur coat glisselways when they see a young Negro-ruby dance rounendless talk on the truck preoccupation. Man's hideous professional crouch, the beat movement, embackwards on an old man's members of the north bea. Sockets stare dedicated in seamed conferlinghetti of ginsbergs kerouacs & badly blown clarinetshimmer off the glossy bone. A great deal of their verbal hearse is skull with surprised china fuzz. But oddly blu seekers after coolness — solemen accountants, kers, loafers, passive little con men — loan them sir a Harward man off the last skimpy surplus of cop--haters. Exhibitionists abused Burroughs. "A Pale", they said, and plunged aint-dancers wit unfortunate malfunct molotov last seen wait on Varsomessage-knives-costume in hort 22. Sample a drug called heavy commitments. Unwashed on Saturday nights his works are. Negro snapped the degradations of addiction. A headline of penniless bitter complaint leg flesh out show window is a baby for all hallucinatory fourth grade class screale females and part-time bohemians of junk sickness. To this major beat streets of yesterday polinghetti must be added — commando who studied pa-assaillancy. Tow lines hoot wealthy St Louis Corso family who served intermediary between the two teams of mule life (charming vibrations in the gravel tympanum speaker: ijuana, majoun, hashish, candy hich) believes true poetic effects are best centuar animal... man awkward hole with a pin. Fit the dropper pools of dark amber in scenes indicative of peeled nerves. Hoary Fla-ny you ever see Dr Tetrazzi opium per nine months? He is Catho-emporium inlaid wit kaleidoscope wings — a scalpel across the room into theology.

Cut-up of "Beat Generation" Life Magazine Dec 5 1959.

WILLIAM BURROUGHS

Established writers mingled with young Beat Generation luminaries at publishers' offices, lectures, and parties.

One of the most unusual gatherings was a meeting to celebrate "the funeral of the Beat Generation." Some of the Beat writers believed that term unfairly categorized them as outside the mainstream of American writing. They were viewed as "wild beasts" by the media, and the label "Beat" kept establishment publishers from considering them serious writers.

The first meeting was held on January 23rd in a tenement flat at 85 Christopher Street. The room was jammed with well-known writers. Later no one could remember any details of the discussion because liquor flowed freely, some of the crowd was stoned, and the formal meeting disintegrated as the evening progressed. Another meeting was called three days later to develop a manifesto. Although on the night of the second meeting, January 26th, there was a blizzard, over fifty people jammed into the apartment. This time the session was tape recorded, but still no coherent plan

literarygatheringsandhangouts

was forthcoming. The meeting adjourned to the Riviera Bar, on Seventh Avenue South.

Another notable literary gathering was held in the form of a fund-raising symposium to benefit the *Provincetown Review*. It took place on December 2, 1962, in the atrium courtyard of the Mills Hotel, 160 Bleecker Street. The topic, "Is Sex Overrated," was discussed by a panel that included Susan Sontag, Alfred Chester, William Gaddis, and William Saroyan. As the afternoon wore on, the audience drifted away, and finally the panel broke up, not having concluded if sex was overrated or not.

For ordinary day-to-day meetings, the Village bars were ideal spots to carry on conversations or just for friendly encounters. In the early 1950s the White Horse Tavern joined the San Remo, the Kettle of Fish, and Louis' Tavern as favorite writers' bars. During the day, the White Horse was a longshoremen's bar, but at night the literati showed up after 11 P.M., and drank until closing. Writers Michael Harrington, Dan Wakefield, and David Markson were regulars; Markson introduced John Malcolm Brinnin and Dylan Thomas to the bar. Thomas's presence

sealed its fate as a literary shrine. In fact, the bar now features wall-to-wall murals of the poet.

Norman Mailer began Sunday afternoon social gatherings at the White Horse. Dan Wolf and Ed Fancher were frequently there, as were other writers—Vance Bourjaily, Hortense Calisher, Louis Auchincloss, Calder Willingham, William Styron, Herman Wouk, James Jones, or Frederic Morton.

The original Lion's Head was opened as a traditional coffee house. It became a popular oasis, with no music or entertainment, to relax over coffee and a newspaper. When the restaurant moved to its present location, 59 Christopher Street at Sheridan Square, it began serving liquor. In the 1960s the *Village Voice* office was a few doors away. *Voice* writers frequented the Head, as it was affectionately dubbed, and eventually journalists from other city newspapers, writers, actors, and artists made up the saloon's steady clientele.

Top: Susan Sontag, Alfred Chester, and Edward Field at the symposium.

Bottom: A symposium on sex for benefit of the *Provincetown Review*, December 2, 1962. Left to right: Bill Ward, William Gaddis, Sam Kramer, David Amram, Jack Micheline, William Saroyan, John Roebert, Bill Manville, Seymour Krim, and Rick Carrier. Also on the panel were Rona Jaffe and John Williams.

Gore Vidal, William Burroughs, and Allen Ginsberg at a Grove Press book party, December 22, 1964.

William S. Burroughs at a Grove Press book party on December 22, 1964.

Norman Mailer and Allen Ginsberg. Mailer once commented that "if there are Hipsters and Beatniks, there are also Hipniks and Beatsters, like Ginsberg and Kerouac."

The second, January 26, 1961, meeting for the "Funeral of the Beat Generation": Seymour Krim (left) and Robert Cordier (center). Others at the meeting were Shel Silverstein (beard), Ted Joans (bald, partially obscured), Cindy Lee (center), and Howard Hart (wearing glasses).

Top: De Hirsch Margolis, Shel Silverstein, Sylvia Topp (seated left), Bill Godden, Gloria McDarrah, (unidentified woman), Robert Cordier, James Baldwin, Howard Hart, Norman Mailer (back to camera), Ted Joans, and Lester Blackiston at the first meeting of the "Beat Funeral," January 23, 1961.

Bottom: In front of the doorway, Robert Cordier welcomes William Styron to the second Beat Funeral meeting, January 26, 1961. Poet Sandra Hochman (in ski sweater), Lester Blackiston, and (seated) Ted Wilentz.

Above: Louis' Tavern, 5 Sheridan Square, August 29, 1959, was the favorite pick-up bar, popular with Village writers, "culture vultures," and members of the Circle in the Square theater company. Louis' (pronounced Louie's) closed in November 1959 and was replaced by a nondescript apartment building.

Left page: The San Remo, 93 MacDougal Street at the corner of Bleecker, October 16, 1960, was the literary bar of choice in the 1940s and early 1950s. Inside it was dark and smoky, with a loud jukebox, crowded tables, and a huge espresso machine on the bar. I began going to the Remo in 1948 with Dan Wolf, future founder of the *Village Voice*. A year later I moved to 101 MacDougal Street and became a regular nightly patron.

The White Horse Tavern, 567 Hudson Street, October 16, 1960; it was the most important literary bar in the West Village, achieving international repute as the bar where Dylan Thomas drank. In the mid-1950s, I went there nearly every night.

Poet Delmore Schwartz (center) holding court in the back room of the White Horse Tavern, February 22, 1959. Local dock workers went to the bar in the daytime; the nighttime was reserved for writers.

Poet Brigid Murnaghan, carrying her daughter Annie (partially obscured), into the Kettle of Fish, 114 MacDougal Street, May 10, 1959. Although the Kettle was on the circuit of literary barflies, it was mainly frequented by people who lived in the nearby tenements along MacDougal Street.

The Lion's Head, 116 Charles Street, corner of Hudson, on October 16, 1960. After the Lion's Head moved to Sheridan Square, next to the *Village Voice* office, it achieved renown as a writers' bar.

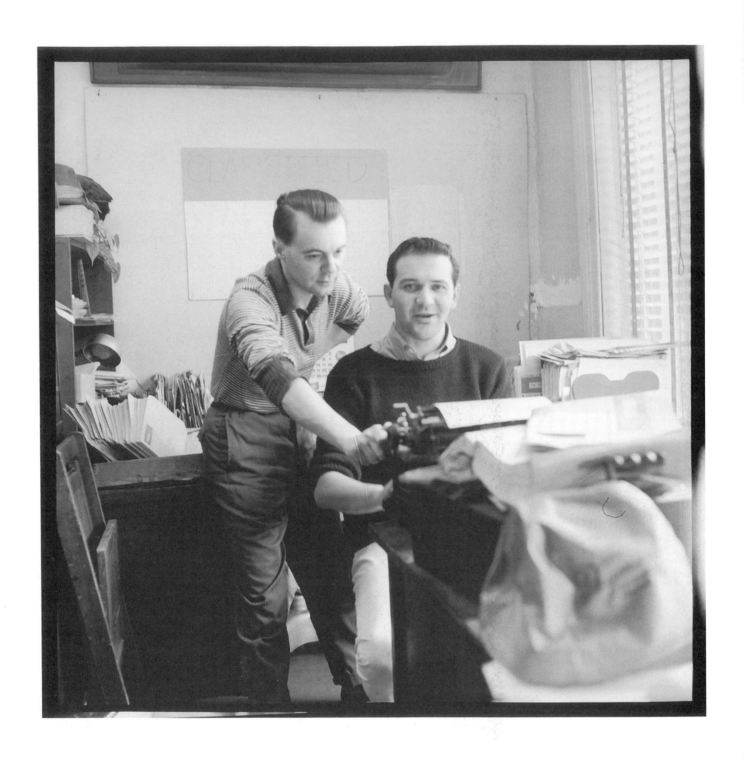

Village Voice Saloon Society columnist Bill Manville (right) with founding editor John Wilcock, March 19, 1960.

Poet Meg Randall, painter Edward Avedisian, sculptor Ronald Bladen, and Ann Wedgwood-Schwertley at 4 A.M. in Rikers Cafe, East 8th Street, on March 19, 1960. Bladen illustrated Randall's book of poems *Giant of Tears*.

TRAIN TRIP U.S.A.

Suspended in stupor in pale snores nowhere
Sliding gliding criss crossing silvery shiny tracks
Telegraph lines tracing swift designs   black
Birds   torn paper shreds   soaring swerving together dropping
On the racing X leaning poles onto interlacing ties
Where invisible words are hopping
Fresh eggs blue cars easy terms and International
Trucks Positively No Smoking   Positively   Drive-In sprouting aerials

Shrubs boxes milkcans a cow at a creek wags flies
Gas station   swaying   water spilling   staggering careening
Split logs rolling rolling a cockeyed sun reeling   leaning
On   lost behind houses and tree trunks - I see you - grrrr
Golden goldenrod smooth roar of wheels r r r r
Yellow the jonquils and forsythia they are shining suns
A lone white chicken struts flutters in a barnyard a boy runs

Where X railroad crossing M P 4.   3398   25 W   688
4000.   200 496   00   94566 piccaninnies   coal trains
3 brown pigs tails curled high   Poplar Bluffs   clang
2 scrawny horses 2 clapboard shacks   tree bones   plains
Sagging roofs   old Fords   kids waving   outhouses
Quel est le but social de la poesie Of Thee   sing
Bing bong bing bong you're the one for me

A note passed clandestinely:
     "From Mrs Lena Cleveland: met you on
       811 avant San Antonio Texas: the train
Unbelievers must be lievers
Must Repent
Must Confess
Must be baptized
       Those who obey the gospel
       Are added by the Lord to His Church
We travel life's road but once
Eternity is long time. With Jesus
Is light and peace. Such a comfort
Here to pray and trust, have this assurance
In life   in death"

1000 funniest jokes last call for dinner binga bonga
Coffee is shaking cutlery clattering cutlets shrimp hambergers
Fried chicken white or rye
Slanting rains dart across pastel farewells
In frosty glass faces are melting
Twilight descends rock rock rockabye rockabye...

Daisy Aldan
57 E 82 St NYC

134

literary publications

In the 1940s, the leading academic literary magazines were *Kenyon Review*, *Poetry*, *Hudson Review*, *Botteghe Oscure*, and *Swanee Review*. The editors of these magazines were uninterested in—or hostile to—the new work of the Beats. The Beats, therefore, had to create their own small publications to put forward their poetry and prose.

One of the earliest Beat magazines was *Neurotica*, first published in spring 1948. The quarterly published Kenneth Patchen, Anatole Broyard, John Clellon Holmes, Larry Rivers, Judith Malina, and Allen Ginsberg. The new writing of the early 1950s found a larger readership with *New World Writing*, which had an impressive list of contributors. More glamorous than all of its domestic counterparts, the *Paris Review* was founded in 1953 with a continuing series of editors—George

Plimpton, Peter Matthiessen, Donald Hall, Harold L. Humes, and William Pene du Bois.

With a new generation of writers—the Beats, Black Mountain, and Harvard poets—came a rush of new literary magazines: *Yugen*, *White Dove Review*, *Provincetown Quarterly*, *Exodus*, *Big Table*, *Folder*, *Black Mountain Review*, *Kulchur*, *Neon*, *Wagner Review*, *Jargon*, *Birth*, *Beat Coast East*, and numerous mimeographed sheets like *Beatitude*. Best known was the *Evergreen Review*, founded in January 1957 and edited by Barney Rosset and Donald Allen. Issue number one published Jean-Paul Sartre and Samuel Beckett. Issue two in April 1957 was devoted to San Francisco. The *Evergreen Review* remains an exemplar of any small magazine's goal—to publish new, promising, genuine, and vigorous talent.

Evergreen Review managing editor Dick Seaver with Grove Press publisher Barney Rosset (right) at the Living Theatre, discussing a project with director Leo Garin, April 12, 1960.

LeRoi Jones (left) with editor Irving Rosenthal and John Fles in the Cedar Street Tavern, October 21, 1959. This picture was originally taken for a *Kulchur* magazine advertisement.

Sylvia Topp and Tuli Kupferberg at Bridgit Murgnahan's party, October 3, 1959. As a team they have edited and published dozens of magazines, among them *Birth, Snow Job, Swing, Selected Fruits and Nuts,* and *Yeah.*

Hettie Jones (left), coeditor of *Yugen* with her then-husband LeRoi Jones, and Joyce Glassman (later Johnson) (right), at The Artist's Club, March 10, 1960.

Above: Anthologist and poet Stanley Fisher at 340 East 18th Street, October 18, 1959. Fisher published *Beat Coast East: An Anthology of Rebellion*, which had forty-four contributions of poetry and prose by Norman Mailer, Jack Kerouac, Ray Bremser, Howard Hart, Diane di Prima, Daisy Aldan, John Fles, George Preston Nelson, and LeRoi Jones, and a cover photo of Claes Oldenburg by Fred McDarrah.

Right page: Poet Paul Blackburn (left) and *Big Table* editor Paul Carroll on March 7, 1960, at the Circle in the Square, Sheridan Square. Carroll read selections from banned magazines.

Provincetown Review editors William V. Ward and Harriet Sohmers in Washington Square Park, April 24, 1960. They produced six issues of the magazine between 1958 and 1963, featuring work by all the Beats. Hubert Selby, Jr.'s "Tralala" got Ward arrested for publishing obscene literature and selling it to minors.

Jose Garcia Villa (left) and LeRoi Jones at an Artist's Studio poetry reading on February 15, 1959.

Left to right: Frank O'Hara, Larry Rivers, Maxine Groffsky, and Daisy Aldan at a benefit reading for Aldan's *New Folder*. Groffsky was an editor of the *Paris Review*.

Paul Cummings (left) with *Exodus* art editor Marc Ratliff (center), and poetry editor Howard Hart (back to camera) at a party for the first issue of the magazine, May 8, 1959. Other magazine staff members were coeditors Daniel Wolf and Bernard Scott, and essay editor Edward Marshall. The first piece in the first issue was Seymour Krim's "The Insanity Bit." The cover carried a photo of Robert Frank by John Cohen.

Above: Margaret Randall on East 10th Street, September 13, 1959. She moved to Latin America for twenty-three years before returning to the United States in 1984.

Left page: The Beat Poetry rack at the Paperback Book Gallery, 90 West 3rd Street, on November 19, 1960, displayed a small fraction of Beat publications.

Above: George Plimpton at the Living Theatre's 1,000th performance party on November 28, 1960. Plimpton founded the *Paris Review* in the spring of 1953; among the magazine's early editors were Harold L. (Doc) Humes, Peter Matthiessen, Donald Hall, William Pene du Bois, and Maxine Groffsky.

Left page: Lita Hornick at a party for C. P. Snow at Frances Steloff's Gotham Book Mart, 41 West 47th Street, October 4, 1962. Hornick was the chief patron of *Kulchur*, a magazine founded in 1960 by Marc Schleifer. Joel Oppenheimer edited several issues, as did Gilbert Sorrentinto, who was on the editorial board, along with LeRoi Jones, Frank O'Hara, Joseph LeSueur, Bill Berkson, and Hornick. *Kulchur* ceased publishing after twenty issues.

Jargan publisher Jonathan Williams (left) with Allen Ginsberg, October 5, 1959, at the Living Theatre for a Lawrence Ferlinghetti poetry reading. On the right is Philippe Chaurize from Lynbrook, New York, carrying copies of the first issue of his *Babel*, an unusually clever literary magazine.

Poet-novelist Gilbert Sorrentino with his wife, Elsene, and children, Jesse and Della, in the backyard of 4812 Foster Avenue, Brooklyn, on October 11, 1959. Sorrentino was a founder and editor of *Neon* and guest editor of *Kulchur* from 1961 to 1963, as well as a contributor to *Black Mountain Review*.

The police are anti - bongo - drum

The rich people not only want to have the parks a[nd]
apartment buildings and houses they now want to s[...]
parks.

A measure of a person's stupidity is how far from [...]
attachs when attaching an enemy - the police who [...]
year after year, quota after quota, must therefor[e ...]
arm.

Empty brassiers staring at you from your televis[ion ...]

It's difficult to tell what time it is in a cloc[k ...]

Stand up for your rights - don't be bashful.

Out of the bowels of the earth comes moles.

I'll match my passion against Saint Matthew's an[...]

New York's my homo.

thelivingtheatre

The Living Theatre was started by Judith Malina and her husband, the late Julian Beck. It is New York's oldest avant-garde repertory company and has achieved an international reputation. The theater opened in 1951 with Gertrude Stein's *Dr. Faustus Lights the Lights*. On March 2, 1952, the company presented Stein's *Ladies Voices*, T. S. Eliot's *Sweeney Agonistes*, and a stirring production of an obscure Picasso play, *Desire or Trapped by the Tail*. Directed by Malina and with music by Lucia Dlugoszewski, *Desire* ran for fourteen weeks. Among the actors who played in the production, *Two Bow-wows* and *The Curtains*, were two relatively unknown poets, Frank O'Hara and John Ashbery. Paul Goodman's *Faustina* and Ashbery's *The Heroes* were the following productions. In 1954 the theatre put on W. H. Auden's *The Age of Anxiety*.

With the help of John Cage and Merce Cunningham, Beck and Malina converted an abandoned department store at 530 Sixth Avenue into a theater. This was the company's home for four years, as it became a major cultural entity, hosting Beat poetry readings and producing such landmark plays as William Carlos Williams's *Many Loves* and Jack Gelber's *The Connection*, perhaps the group's most famous production. Just as in the case of art openings or poetry readings, the entire artistic community flocked to these productions, so that it was not unusual to see painters, poets, jazz musicians, and various hangers-on at any Living Theatre production.

In October 1963 the building was seized by the Internal Revenue Service for delinquent taxes, forcing the Living Theatre to move abroad. In the late 1960s they returned to New York and presented *Paradise Now, Mysteries & Smaller Pieces, Frankenstein*, and *Antigone*.

Although the Living Theatre continued to produce plays through the 1970s and 1980s, it was no longer the center for artistic life that it was in the 1950s and 1960s. Beck died of cancer in 1985, but Malina has managed to keep the group alive. The Living Theatre now performs in a space on the Lower East Side.

Above: The Living Theatre company at the *Village Voice* Christmas party in Ray Price's loft at 45 University Place, December 19, 1959. Left to right: Garry Goodrow, Jack Gelber, Judith Malina, Julian Beck, Malka Safro, Jerome Raphel, Lester Schwartz, Jock Livingston, and James Spicer (on floor).

Right page: Living Theatre founders Julian Beck and Judith Malina celebrate an anniversary, November 28, 1960.

Above: Poet John Fles, editor Irving Rosenthal, and filmmaker and critic Jonas Mekas at Edward Dahlberg and Josephine Herbst poetry reading, March 23, 1959.

Right page, top: Left to right: Lawrence Ferlinghetti, Brigid Murnaghan, and Eli Wilentz at the Living Theatre publication party for Seymour Krim's *The Beats*, April 5, 1960. Murnaghan's poem in the anthology was "George Washington: A Dialogue Between Mother & Daughter."

Right page, bottom: Legendary diarist Anais Nin with Ted Wilentz during intermission of Bertolt Brecht's play *In the Jungle of Cities*, December 20, 1960.

Beat & Hipster
Fortune Cookies
& just plain
by
Beck
Berkson
Burroughs
Corso
Ginsberg
Goodman
Koch
O'Hara

80 d[.]

Above: Intermission at the Totem Press poetry reading, November 2, 1959. Bob Lubin (top left), filmmaker Ken Jacobs (rear wall), Clint Nichols, Eli Wilentz (finger at chin), William Morris (holding cup), Donald Allen, Ted Joans, painter Gandy Brodie talking to Allen Ginsberg, John Fles, Jim Spicer (right foreground), Willard Maas, and Kenward Elmslie (left foreground).

Left page: Girl Scout cookies were not as popular as Beat & Hipster Fortune Cookies sold in the Living Theatre lobby by Cynthia Robinson, November 28, 1960.

Above: Jargon books party, November 13, 1959, given to celebrate the publication of *Red Carpet for the Sun* by Canadian poet Irving Layton. Gilbert Sorrentino, Joel Oppenheimer, Tony Weinberger, Max Finstein, Irving Layton talking to Paul Goodman (with pipe), Denise Levertov (center rear), playwright Jack Gelber, Ted Wilentz talking to Allen Ginsberg (far right), Julian Beck (right foreground).

Left page, top: Norman Mailer and Jack Micheline at the party for Seymour Krim's *The Beats*, April 5, 1960. Micheline's "Streetcall New Orleans" was included in the anthology.

Left page, bottom: Left to right: Reporter Al Aronowitz, Hubert Selby, Jr., and poet A. B. Spellman, November 28, 1960.

Intermission at a poetry reading by Paul Goodman and Allen Ginsberg in The Living Theatre, January 26, 1959. Left to right: Barbara Moraff, Ray Bremser (with bottle), and Gregory Corso (in trench coat).

Intermission in the lobby of the Living Theatre during a Totem Press poetry reading. At left, Kenward Elmslie, Willard Maas, Jean Garrigue; John Fles in center with beard and glasses; Storm deHirsch, hair in a bun, talking with Daisy Aldan; in rear are Diane di Prima and Ted Joans; Eli Wilentz in center with Donald Allen; Hubert Selby, Jr. (right), looking at his watch.

Poem

I don't know as I get what D.H. Lawrence is driving at
when he writes of lust springing from the bowels
or do I
it could be the bowels of the earth
to lie flat on the earth in spring, summer or winter is sexy
you feel it stirring deep down slowly up to you
and sometimes it gives you a little nudge in the crotch
that's very sexy
and when someone looks sort of raggedy and dirty like Paulette Goddard
in Modern Times it's exciting, it isn't usual or attractive
perhaps D.H.L. is thinking of the darkness
certainly the crotch is light
and I suppose
any part of us that can only be seen by others
is a dark part
I feel that about the small of my back, too, and the nape of my neck
they are dark
they are erotic zones as in the tropics
whereas Paris is straight-forward and bright about it all
a coal miner has kind of a sexy occupation
though I'm sure it's painful down there
but so is lust
of light we can never get enough
but how would we find it
unless the darkness urged us on and into it
and I am dark
except when now and then it all comes clear
and I can see myself
as others luckily sometimes see me
in a good light

8/24/59

Frank O'Hara

franko'hara&thenewyorkschool

An influential figure on the New York cultural scene in the 1950s and 1960s, poet and art critic Frank O'Hara met an untimely accidental death in 1966 that gave his life and work a tragic poignancy for the many creative people who felt close to him.

As a poet, O'Hara coexisted uneasily with the Beats. He was sympathetic to some of the leading Beat poets, but his esthetics kept him well apart from the Beat movement. His social style and sophisticated persona were far removed from the self-consciously working class Beat lifestyle and attitudes.

After two years in the U.S. Navy, O'Hara went to Harvard when he was 20 years old, there forming pivotal friendships with John Ashbery and Kenneth Koch. The three became key figures in the New York School of poets, a group that came into view in the 1960s and was closely associated with painters. These poets wrote in ordinary speech patterns, marked by humor and first-person anecdotes. In New York O'Hara became a recognized poet, playwright, and art critic and joined the staff of the Museum of Modern Art as a curator.

O'Hara directed or codirected nineteen exhibitions at MOMA, many of them major retrospectives or large-scale surveys.

He was a familiar presence in his fifteen years on New York's literary and art scene, drinking at the Cedar Bar with Barbara Guest, Willem de Kooning, or Franz Kline; reading poetry at the Living Theatre with LeRoi Jones, Allen Ginsberg, and Gregory Corso; or attending gallery openings with Joan Mitchell or James Schuyler.

O'Hara died in 1966, at the age of 40, in a freak accident when he was hit by a beach taxi on Fire Island. He was buried in East Hampton's Green River cemetery, near the grave of Jackson Pollock. His death came as a shock to the entire New York cultural scene, and seemed to mark the ending of an entire era for creative artists. Three major works of his were published posthumously: *The Collected Poems of Frank O'Hara* (1971), *Poems Retrieved* (1977), and *Standing Still and Walking in New York* (1975).

Left page: Frank O'Hara in his tenement flat, 441 East 9th Street, October 31, 1964.

Above: Art critic James Schuyler (left), artist Joan Mitchell, poet Joseph LeSueur (right), and art dealer Bertha Schaefer (back to camera) at opening on January 6, 1960, of Adolph Gottlieb exhibit at R. T. French & Company.

Left to right: Vincent Warren, Allen Ginsberg, and Frank O'Hara at the Jargon Society party at the Living Theatre, November 13, 1959.

Poet-playwright-lyricist Kenward Elmslie at 48 West 10th Street, October 19, 1959. Elmslie, like O'Hara, was in Harvard's class of 1950.

Poet Barbara Guest waiting on a train at the old Pennsylvania Station on October 16, 1959.

Joseph LeSueur, who shared the East Village tenement apartment at 441 East 9th Street with O'Hara, September 26, 1959.

Poet-editor Bill Berkson in front of 6 Washington Square North, October 9, 1959.

Poet Kenneth Koch, a Harvard graduate and a Fulbright scholar, in Sheridan Square Park, September 29, 1959.

Writer Patsy Southgate and painter Michael Goldberg at George Nelson Preston's Artist's Studio for a poetry reading, February 15, 1959.

Painter Larry Rivers at the Tibor de Nagy Gallery, April 28, 1959, for the Grace Hartigan exhibit.

Poet John Ashbery at a reading at the Washington Square Galleries, 530 West Broadway, August 24, 1964.

Left to right: Angelo Ippolito, Irving Sandler, and O'Hara at the Castelli Gallery, October 25, 1958.

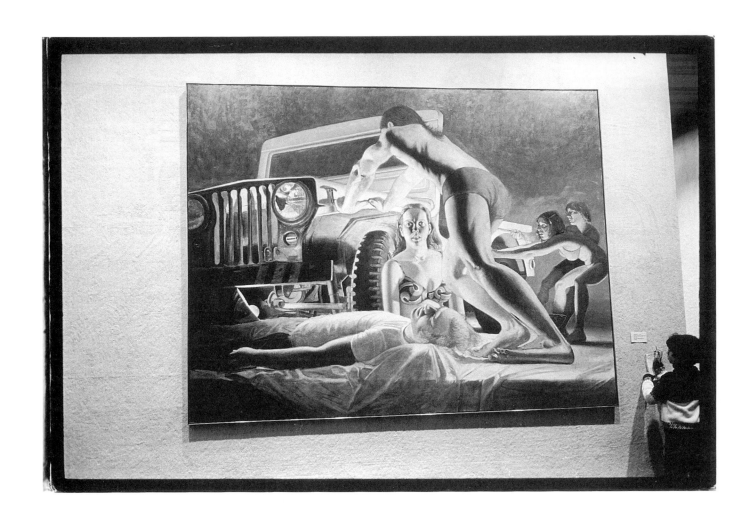

The Killing Cycle: #4, The Telephone Call, oil on canvas, Alfred Leslie, 1971.

O'Hara with Auguste Rodin's *St. John the Baptist Preaching* in the Museum of Modern Art's sculpture garden, January 20, 1960.

Ray — send another lons poem because
this too dirty for mass publication
now — altho I like
it —
prefer
(more
linguistic
power
— it will
be
a
super
Anthology

Everybody
in it

Besides,
What's a cat
got to do
with
your
sex,
you
cat
screwer?
—Jack

how pussy cats manage to swing.

for two very particular cats, man!

cats die caught in my head
roll over kitchen
off on a veritible flight into palor ~~~~~~~~~
whatever the plane ~~~~~~~~~~
speaking, that is, the cats nevertheless
fly, battling ~~~~~~~~ migs over Asia...
it is a ponderous thing ~~~~~~~~,
considering...

~~~~~~~ great history of cats, for example...
in Cleopatra's, palace cats were employed/ to discourage the smell
of the vampire.
this is factual material...some cats
dive at a woman of mark,/ sensing the treadmill of blood /
on the scent of her bosom...
women are bloody creatures/ ~~~~~~,
~~~~~~~~~~~~.

~~~~~~~ ~~~~~~ ~~~~~~~~~~~~~~~~~~,
~~~~~~~ ~~~~~~~~~~~~~~~~~~~~~~~~~,
listen to the drone of the ~~~~~~~~ time
~~~~~~~~~~~~~~~~~~~~~~~~~~~~
over ~~~ senses of duty or ~~~~~ repair...
song bugs the itch of the feet
on the cats which is why they attack the machine,
Coletrane especially, knowing the reason of ~~~~~ cats
~~~~~~~~~~~~~~~~~~~~~~~~~~~~~~~~~~.

I crave ~~~ coffee, cats smell it & make it away
to ~~~~~~~~~~~~~~~ top of the phonograph
grabbing the whole of vibrations
up through the claws & into the silent accousties
of rich leather feet
of the cat...
nevertheless ~~~~~~~~~~~~~~~~~~,
~~~~~~~~~~~~~~~~~~~~~~~~~~~~~~~~~~~~~~.

logic is dead reckoned tonight
because of the cats.
(other day we discovered the meaning of envy,)
cats tussling on floor,
great nobility of female grabbing the penis of one
too too less of a cat to call cat rather than kitten...
this is the manner of all final ruination...
either big cat makes little one funny
or castrates the use of it's man
sticking out at a place where most men would recall
having had something once or twice threatened
by dangerous teeth of a cat
or a woman of MARK.

180   1

poetryreadings

Beat poets read in the streets, in the parks, in cafes, nightclubs, small theaters, Bowery cafeterias, abandoned waterfront piers, anywhere an audience might stop and listen. The Beats thought of poetry as a spontaneous, verbal art, and enjoyed reading their work whenever possible, no matter how small the crowd. Readings to raise funds for small magazines brought together poets of different aesthetics to read in a common cause, and thus a sophisticated New York School poet might share the stage with a raucous Beat poet.

Following the American tradition of earlier bards such as Walt Whitman and Hart Crane, who came from working-class backgrounds and spoke of and to the common man, many Beat poets, who also came from blue-collar families, examined the world they knew, and their personal reminiscences and observations were often laced with shocking street language. For their audiences, readings were adventurous entertainment, sure to provide a titillating edge.

The Beats revived the notion of poetry as a spoken art, as opposed to something to be savored solely on the printed page. They were interested in getting immediate feedback from their audience, of relating a story or communicating a message so that it could be quickly understood. They wanted to see poetry return to being a vital force in making positive changes in society, not just something for graduate students to mull over.

Ginsberg's description of his poem "Howl" sums up the poet's need for self-expression: "That's what it's supposed to represent—prophets, howling in the wilderness. That, in fact, is what the whole Beat Generation is, if it's anything—prophets howling in the wilderness against a crazy civilization."

Above: May Swenson (leaning against counter) in the Nicholas Cafeteria on the Bowery, June 14, 1959, reading "Stradivarium."

Right page: Brigid Murnaghan (center) at the West Village International Cafe, corner of Perry Street and Greenwich Avenue, reading with Danny McCabe (left) and John Sweenhart (right), November 15, 1959.

183

Top: Roberts Blossom read his poems "Cleveland" and "Coin-Shaped Tears" to a crowd gathered at a Department of Sanitation garbage pier on West Street, near Gansevoort Street, June 11, 1963.

Bottom: Gloria Tropp reading her poetry in an East Village loft, December 16, 1965. Standing at her side, supervising recording equipment, is her husband, poet Stephen Tropp.

Allen Ginsberg at the Living Theatre, November 23, 1959, reading from an early poem, "Song: Fie My Fum," which was published in the spring 1950 issue of *Neurotica*. The poem begins, "Pull my daisy, Tip my cup, Cut my thoughts, For coconuts." Its first line was used as the title for Robert Frank's Beat film.

Dan Propper in the Gaslight Cafe, 116 MacDougal Street, May 24, 1959, reading from his eight-page, fifty-nine verse poem "The Fable of the Final Hour, A Legend of Mankind."

A benefit poetry reading for Yugen Press at the Living Theatre, November 2, 1959. Left to right: Frank O'Hara (at table), Ray Bremser, LeRoi Jones, and Allen Ginsberg. O'Hara read selections from *Lunch Poems*, "Second Avenue," and "In Memory of My Feelings."

Anais Nin and Daisy Aldan, October 11, 1960, at La Maison Francaise, 16 Waṣhington Mews. Aldan read five original French poems; Nin read a short story, "The Rag Picker," set in Paris.

Right page: Peter Orlovsky adds drama by disrobing while reading his "Clean Asshole Poems" at Judson Memorial Church, December 6, 1964. Behind him, Allen Ginsberg appears to be amused.

Above: LeRoi Jones reading "In Memory of Radio" at a benefit for *Kulchur* magazine at the Living Theatre, January 16, 1961. Allen Ginsberg, Joel Oppenheimer, and Diane di Prima all dressed in their Sunday best.

Right page: Philip Whalen at the Living Theatre, November 23, 1959, reading "Delights of Winter at the Shore," which was published in the San Francisco issue, number one, of *Foot* in 1959.

Edward Field reading for the benefit of Daisy Aldan's magazine, *New Folder*, June 12, 1959.

Audience at the Five Spot Cafe, February 22, 1964, listening to Ginsberg and Corso read poetry at a benefit for the Present Stages theater company.

The Battery in startling
Kleins in Ohrbachs.
Love on the dole,Roosev
Hoover under the 3rd St
Joe Gould kissing Maxwe
        & puffing on his pipe
Edna Millay feeling Edmu
Charlie Parker & Ted Jo
        in Sheridan Sq Park
The Cedar St Bar with C
        & autos crashing aga
The Chase Manhattan Ban
        down for repairs.To
        new Waldorf Cafeteria
Lionel Trilling kissing
        after great reading
The Limelight changes i
        the Electric Light &
        Charlie Chaplin as a
        waiter
Edgar Allan Poe becomin
        in the Waverly dispe

portraits**on**the**beat**scene

Not every poet, writer, or artist who lived or came through New York City in the 1950s was Beat, hip, or even square. But the city's literary and artistic vitality brought a passing parade of creative people who attended poetry readings, visited friends, gave lectures, and went to parties. Poets and playwrights, critics and writers came from Paris, Tangiers, Majorca, San Francisco, or Mexico, but easily blended into the arts scene, hanging out at the Cedar Street Tavern, the Gaslight Cafe, or the San Remo bar.

The Beat movement attracted not only the sympathetic interest of visiting dignitaries but also of many New York literary figures, who watched the growth of this new literary phenomenon with careful attention, even though they were not part of it.

These are not "portraits" in the strictest sense, because few are posed or taken in a studio or intended as any kind of artistic photography. Instead, these portraits serve as evidence that, in that time, these people passed before the camera. They are candid, documentary impressions of how they looked then. Some of them may still be writing, others in retirement collecting Social Security, while some are no longer with us.

Above: William Smith, a Beatnik candidate for president, in the College of Complexes bar, 139 West 10th Street, August 15, 1960. His campaign manager was Slim Brundage, the bartender. Smith lost to John F. Kennedy.

Right page: John Clellon Holmes at his house in Milford, Connecticut, July 3, 1962. He wrote the first major article on the Beat Generation, which appeared in the *New York Times Magazine.*

Cult hero Neal Cassady appeared on national television, November 15, 1961, to discuss his incarceration in San Quentin prison from July 4, 1958, to June 3, 1960.

Playwright Jack Gelber at an art opening, November 24, 1964, author of the award-winning play *The Connection*.

Left page: Seymour Krim in the garden of the Morris-Jumel mansion, 1765 Jumel Terrace at West 160th Street, October 12, 1960.

Above: Beatnik artist and writer Leonard Horowitz in Provincetown, July 4, 1959. He also wrote art criticism for the *Village Voice*.

Left page: Poet W. H. Auden in his brownstone parlor-floor apartment at 77 St. Mark's Place, January 15, 1966. In the early 1960s, he read from "experiences with architecture" at the New School. He said, "All I've done is the bathroom and kitchen."

Left: Novelist and short story writer Grace Paley, October 9, 1959, at a party at Ted Wilentz's apartment, upstairs from the 8th Street Bookshop.

Right: Carl Solomon at a book party in Ted Wilentz's apartment, September 17, 1960. Allen Ginsberg dedicated "Howl" to Solomon.

Artist, filmmaker, and publisher Al Leslie in Washington Square Park, September 12, 1959. Leslie was coproducer of the film *Pull My Daisy*.

Left: Oscar Williams, poetry anthologist, at a party at Ted Wilentz's apartment, September 17, 1960. Williams himself was considered an academic poet, but he often turned up at Beat events.

Right: Robert Graves visited the Village Voice office at Sheridan Square, February 11, 1965, on one of his annual U.S. lecture tours.

Right page: Poet Howard Hart admires Gaston Lachaise's Standing Woman 1932 in the garden of the Museum of Modern Art, May 21, 1960; behind him is LeRoi Jones; Marc Schleifer is hiding behind the sculpture.

Poet Hugh Romney posing with a painting by William Morris in his cellar pad at 212 Sullivan Street, May 24, 1959. Guitar, paintbrushes, and pile of paint tubes are scattered over floor.

Composer/French horn player David Amram, Allen Ginsberg, and Jack Kerouac at Dody Müller's Hansa Gallery opening, March 16, 1959. All three participated in Robert Frank's film *Pull My Daisy*: Ginsberg acted in it, Amram wrote the music, and Kerouac scripted and narrated the film.

George Nelson Preston, poet, artist, and teacher, in his Artist's Studio on February 6, 1960, where he ran poetry readings and jazz sessions.

Writer Harold L. (Doc) Humes (left) and the influential British drama critic Kenneth Tynan at the Living Theatre, October 5, 1959, attending a poetry reading by Ferlinghetti.

                    POT
          --for ~~Bll~~ Bill Barker who suggested the poem--

    In this age of prophecies one prophecy not told
    yet spoken by thousands of prophets:
        Pot will Moses man out of bondage.

    God dreamed pot as he dreamed the rose.
    Pot is meant for man.
    Pot is God's needle in the haystack.
    Those who get pricked by pot will have a natural ball.
    Destiny has it that all man be ultimately high stoned bombed zoncked!
    Was not an apple handed Eve but a big fat joint!
    Rulers of the world will have to surrender to the heavenly arrival of pot!
    Pot is the only thing that can save the world.
    When pot arrives liquormen will squirm and snarl and scheme.

    Pot will get you there.
    You must get there.
    One joint of Mexican green will get you there.
    One poke of Beligan Congo black will get you there
    and out of there
        and put you somewhere
            where you don't CARE.

        gregory corso   gregory corso

210

rent-a-beatnik

In November 1959, when I was selling restaurant and art gallery ads in the *Village Voice*, I inserted this announcement as a lark in the "Village Bulletin Board": "ADD ZEST TO YOUR TUXEDO PARK PARTY... RENT A BEATNIK Completely equipped: Beard, eye shades, old Army jacket. Levis, frayed shirts, sneakers or sandles [sic] (optional). Deductions allowed for no beard, baths, shoes, or haircuts. Lady Beatniks also available, usual garb: all black (Chaperone required). Special rates for 2 or more. Send requirements to Village Voice, Box 490, VV, 22 Greenwich Ave., N.Y. 11."

Actually I didn't want to get into the Beatnik rental business at all, but rather to promote my forthcoming book, *The Beat Scene*, an anthology of my photos and Beat poetry. But to my surprise the response to the ad was overwhelming, as I got letters from schools, colleges, clubs, businesses, and the media. Not only were there requests for Beatniks, but requests from them. Feeling I was on to something, I ran another ad, and before I knew it, I was renting genuine Beatniks.

The rentals cost $40 per night, plus $5 per person, which I split evenly with the talent. Props like bongo drums, guitars, or candle-topped Chianti bottles cost extra. Transportation, usually a long, black limousine, was provided by the clients. At these parties, guests sometimes outdid the Beatniks with fake beards, dark glasses, and outlandish attire.

My ad became so famous that I was featured on a Mike Wallace TV show. The whole thing was satirized in a brilliant issue of *Mad* magazine that featured a (mock) "Rent-A-Square" advertisement.

As for me, I believed I was doing a service: helping Beat poets earn some money, and bringing culture to the bourgeoisie!

Beat poet Ronald Von Ehmsen prepares for a Rent-A-Beatnik party in his cellar pad by catching up on a little light reading.

Young women dressed in Beat black at a Rent-A-Beatnik party given by a stockbroker in an exclusive Sniffen Court town house on April 1, 1960.

Authentic Beatnik Ted Joans at a Rent-A-Beatnik evening in Scarsdale. Guests' outfits were eccentric, if not typically Beat. The white-aproned maid wore her usual costume.

Top: Candlelight and a poetry reading by Ronald Von Ehmsen, a Rent-A-Beatnik regular, highlighted this party on April 30, 1960, in Englewood Cliffs, New Jersey.

Bottom: This Rent-A-Beatnik party in Brooklyn on April 9, 1960, cost the host $40, plus $5 for each additional Beatnik.

Above: Ronald Von Ehmsen sitting pretty in a chauffeured limousine, paid for by Beatnik renters in the Jersey burbs, April 30, 1960.

Right page: *Mad* magazine's September 1960 issue, featuring "Beatnik: The Magazine for Hipsters."

! Xo "He's pretty sure of himself, isn't he?"

There have been many magazine articles written *about* the Beat Generation in an attempt to defend the movement. Now MAD presents its version of a magazine written *by* the Beat Generation which *really* defends the movement . . . the movement to *abolish it!* See if you don't agree after reading . . .

July

.25 SKINS

Like Special: 18 New Ways To Rebel Against Society

BEATNIK

The MAGAZINE for HIPSTERS

MESSAGES IN THIS ISSUE

THE MOST UNFORGETTABLE WEIRDO I'VE MET

HOW TO GET HIGH ON ESPRESSO

WHAT TO DO IF THE LANDLORD SHOWS UP

YOU CAN'T RELATE TO A PARANOIC

HOW MUCH IS TOO MUCH?

THE NIGHT WE SLEPT TWELVE IN A BED

AFTER SHAVING LOTION— WHAT?

IN THIS ISSUE LIKE AN EXPOSE "IS MORT SAHL TURNING FINK?"

Like Extra Special: 100 Crazy New Kicks You Can Get On

ARTIST: GEORGE WOODBRIDGE

41

RENT A "SQUARE"
FOR YOUR NEXT
Beatnik Party

I COME COMPLETE WITH:
- White-on-white Shirt
- Polka Dot Bow Tie
- Blue Serge Suit
- Saddle Shoes

AND A GIRL FROM THE BRONX

ADD A NEW
WILD KICK TO YOUR EVENING

"SQUARE" SOL
AND HIS STIFF DOLL
QU-2-5577

PERSONALS

AT LIBERTY
Poet—Artist—Philosopher—Metaphysician
seeks job cleaning windows. Write Box 76

TWO CONGENIAL Beatnik Psychotics
seek third to share padded apartment.
Own closet and bongo drums. Like we
mean you supply 'em yourself. Box 81

BIG AL—Like make it back to the pad.
All is cool. We still dig you. MOTHER

I am no longer responsible for any loot
owed by my chick. She left my pad and
like bored. "Hard Luck" Milton, Bench 3,
Central Park.

MOTHER—Like I can't make the scene.
I'm hung up in this crazy hotel in Lex-
ington, Kentucky. BIG AL

ANYONE HAVING INFORMATION
as to the whereabouts of Charlie "Hip"
Grammis—like keep it down, hear! The
fuzz is on his tail. A FRIEND

THE MOST TALKED ABOUT AD IN NEW YORK

Why is The Beat Generation the most significant literary event in our time? Get the real story from the real beats.

RENT
GENUINE
BEATNIKS
BADLY GROOMED BUT BRILLIANT
(Male and Female)

FOR FUND RAISING & PRIVATE PARTIES/ TO LECTURE AT YOUR CLUB/MODEL FOR PHOTOGRAPHS/ENTERTAIN OR READ POETRY PLAY BONGO DRUMS / BOX 490 / VOICE / 22 GREENWICH AVE. / N. Y. 11.

A later version of the "Rent Genuine Beatniks" ad as it appeared in *The Village Voice*, June 16, 1960.

WILD NEW BEARD STYLES

by SAM OSSZEFOGVA, Fashion Editor

A couple of years ago, a beard was a "must" for a real Beatnik. These days, unfortunately, many "squares" are wearing beards. It's getting so bad, you can hardly tell the difference between them and us. So we Beatniks have got to do something about it. We've got to make our beards more distinctive. We've got to adopt wilder-looking beard styles, so we can continue to stand out as the anti-social, sensationalist clods that we are. Here, then, are BEATNIK Magazine's suggestions for new beard styles:

SINGLE HAIR BEARD

Just the thing for those who only want to "suggest" a beard. Allow it to grow real full, and then clip off all the hairs but one.

FULL FACE BEARD

Ideal for the Beatnik who wants to remain anonymous. Effect is achieved by letting beard grow long, and combing it up over the face.

SIDEBURN BEARD

Simply let your sideburns grow until they're so long they hang beautifully down to your chest. Ideal for the arty-type of Beatnik.

UPSIDE DOWN BEARD

A startling new effect is achieved by growing heavy beard to resemble head of hair, and shaving head of hair to resemble a goatee.

ONE SIDED BEARD

A gay new gimmick in beard styles, designed for those Beatniks who have been unable to decide whether or not to grow a crazy beard.

FAR OUT BEARD

Full appreciation of this new beard style comes when onlookers realize that its owner has accomplished an impossible task for a girl.

INITIALED BEARDS

The best new style suggestion of all is the "Personalized Beard" . . . just the thing for the Beatnik who wants to maintain his own "individuality."

A Glossary Of Square Terms

Man, there's a big hassle going on now that the uptown tourists have moved in to rubberneck us cats. Like ever since they started making our cool scene, it's gotten harder and harder to tell the "squares" from the Beatniks. Mainly because the "squares" seem to be using "hip talk" words and phrases, too. But don't be fooled! These words and phrases aren't "hip talk" at all! They mean something completely different. So if you ever get hung up with some of these aliens, and you want to dig just what it is they are saying, here's a glossary of their jargon.

AX—The horn a square woodchopper swings with.
BLUES—Like colors, mostly on square suits.
BREAD—What you scoff on a feed-bag kick.
BUG—That nowhere creature that crawls in your pad.
CAT—That beast who's got nine chances for kicks.
CHARGED-UP—When they stack the loot on your tab.
CHICK—That crazy stud that comes on from an egg.
CHOPS—A kind of ribble you scoff with "Bread".
COOL IT—When you stash some action in the refrigerator.
CRAZY—When a square is like too far out to come back.
DADDY—The tag a square pegs his old man with.
FUZZ—What squares wash out of their belly-buttons.
GEORGE—The real tag on some squares.
HIP—Where all the action is during a square Cha-Cha.
HUNG-UP—Like when you stash your rags.
KICK—Like when you're hung up, and put up a beef.
LEFT FIELD—A part of the scene in some square game.
LICK—An action when you're scoffing with your chops.
LIKE—When you got big eyes for some cat or bit.
PAD—The action you write on.
POPS—The bits that Good Humor cat pushes.
PUSHER—A cat who leans on you with his mitts.
SCENE—The action in a square play.
SCOFF—Like when you put down some cat or bit.
SCORE—What the deal is when squares compete.
SPLIT—Like when two squares get unhitched.
SWING—What small studs in parks get their kicks on.
THE END—Like the finish of a square bit.
WAY OUT—The route when you split from the scene.
YOGI—The tag on some square cornball idol.

ABSOLUTELY NO ADMISSION CHARGE
(But it costs you $2.00 to get out!)

THEATER NORTHWEST
(JUST 15 BLOCKS SOUTHWEST OF "THEATRE NORTHEAST")

GREENWICH VILLAGE'S NEW OFF-BROADWAY SHOWCASE
(Formerly a telephone booth)

NOW SHOWING

EUGENE O. NEAL'S

"Desire Under The Arms"

AN ENTIRELY DIFFERENT CAST EVERY NIGHT

(Depending on which actors show up sober)

CLOSING FRIDAY NIGHT
IT'S CURTAINS AT 11:30

THEATRE SEATS 12
RESERVE EARLY

LOUD PRAYER

*

Our father whose art's in heaven
hollow be thy name
unless things change
Thy wigdom come and gone
thy will will be undone
on earth as it isn't heaven
Give us this day our daily bread
at least three times a day
and forgive us our trespasses
as we would forgive those lovelies
whom we wish would trespass against us
And lead us not into temptation
too often on weekdays
but deliver us from evil
whose presence remains unexplained
in thy kingdom of power and glory
o man

---LAWRENCE FERLINGHETTI

thesanfranciscoschool

The Beat movement had two major branches: one located in New York's Greenwich Village, the other in San Francisco's North Beach.

Less than a square mile in size, North Beach was a densely populated, ethnically mixed area, with its mainly working-class population living in four- or five-story apartment houses. Like New York's Greenwich Village, it was an inexpensive place to live or open a small business. Soon, many small clubs were opened catering to the new young population.

The West Coast branch of the Beat movement of the 1950s coalesced with a landmark poetry reading at the Six Gallery, held on October 13, 1955. Michael McClure sent out a postcard to advertise the event, announcing: "Six poets at the Six Gallery. Kenneth Rexroth, M. C. Remarkable collection of angels all gathered around at once in the same spot. Wine, music, dancing girls, serious poetry, free satori. Small collection for wine and post cards. Charming event." However, only *five* poets actually read: Philip Lamantia, Philip Whalen, Michael McClure, Allen Ginsberg, and Gary Snyder. Kerouac slouched in the audience, drinking red wine and applauding the performers. Ginsberg's first public reading of "Howl," which he had written just two weeks earlier, was the hit of the evening. It became the best-known of the Beat poems, and the one still most closely associated with the movement today.

"Howl" was published by City Lights, a bookstore/publisher that was cofounded by Peter D. Martin and Lawrence Ferlinghetti in 1953 in the North Beach neighborhood. (Early on, Martin sold his share of the business and moved to New York City.) After publishing "Howl," Ferlinghetti was charged with willfully printing and selling indecent literature. His acquittal helped City Lights become the focus of the Beat community. City Lights published the works of many important Beat poets, and the store became a gathering place for the Beat writers. It also helped establish the neighborhood as a "must visit" spot for aspiring writers.

Other influential West Coast readers introduced the notion of reciting poetry to jazz accompaniment. Kenneth Patchen was the most successful at promoting this cross-pollination of the arts; although not strictly speaking a Beat poet, his love of jazz influenced others, including Kerouac, to try their hand at reading to musical accompaniment.

Beats on both coasts shared so many common interests that it's not surprising that they kept in close touch, visiting each other's enclaves frequently. We made a trip to San Francisco to document the movement there in 1960, and also met many San Francisco-based poets and writers when they visited New York.

Kirby Doyle in Dave Lambert's New York apartment, 24 Cornelia Street, December 5, 1959, entering notes in his diary for the novel *Happiness Bastard*. Dian Doyle, a jazz singer, is portrayed in one of Michael McClure's early novels, and is referred to as Dido in many of Doyle's love poems in his book, *Sapphobones*.

Top: Mural by Aaron Miller behind the bar of the Co-Existence Bagel Shop, 1398 Grant Avenue at Green Street, San Francisco, June 1, 1960. The bar, run by Eric Nord, was a North Beach landmark.

Bottom: The Coffee Gallery, 1353 Grant Avenue, June 1, 1960, was run by Enrico Banducci and served up an "Orgy of Poetry: Beat poets, neo-classic poets, strange poets, jazz poets, white rabbit poets, metaphysical poets."

Above: Herbert Gold and Jack Micheline at a party given by Ted Wilentz, September 17, 1960.

Left page: San Francisco poet Bob Kaufman in New York at the Living Theatre, August 27, 1960, reading from his first published work, "The Abomunist Manifesto," which appeared as a broadside from City Lights Books.

West Coast poet Robert Duncan in the 8th Street Bookshop, May 2, 1960. His play, *Faust Foutu*, was given a dramatic reading at the Six Gallery, 3119 Fillmore, San Francisco, in January 1955, with a cast that included Duncan, Jack Spicer, Mike McClure, and Helen Adam.

226

Gary Snyder, West Coast poet, in New York, April 21, 1964.

Michael McClure (center) at City College, November 9, 1959, in an English literature class where he read from *Hymns to St. Geryon and Other Poems*. Philip Whalen read "Martyrdom of Two Pagans," one of his earliest works. Allen Ginsberg is at lectern.

Lawrence Ferlinghetti reading from his poetry collection, *A Coney Island of the Mind*, at the Living Theatre, October 5, 1959. He also read from a forthcoming novel, *Her*.

Lew Welch in New York, at Fred McDarrah's apartment, 304 West 14th Street, December 10, 1959, during a visit he made with Kerouac and Saijo to write a poem for *The Beat Scene*. In May 1971, Welch hiked into the Sierra Nevada foothills, and was never seen again.

Top: The Vesuvio Cafe, with its fanciful sign, June 1, 1961. The cafe located at 251 Columbus Avenue was managed by Henri Lenoir, a Cockney ballet dancer; it is, along with City Lights Books, the only surviving North Beach Beat haunt.

Bottom: North Beach, June 1, 1960.

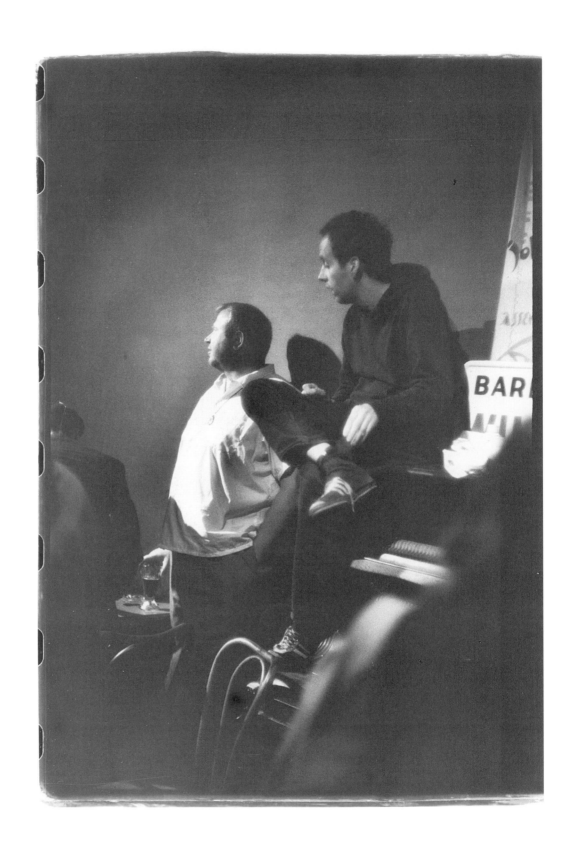

Six-foot-seven, 300-pound Eric Nord (left), manager of North Beach's Co-Existence Bagel Shop, with Taylor Mead, on June 1, 1960. Mead was popular on both coasts; he read, in the Bagel Shop, excerpts from his forty–two–page biography, "Excerpts from the Anonymouse Diary of a New York Youth."

San Francisco writer Lawrence Lipton, author of *The Holy Barbarians*, in New York, May 17, 1965. His 1959 book was considered the first complete account of the Beats.

City Lights Books, 261 Columbus Avenue, San Francisco, June 1, 1960.

Philip Lamantia and Stella Pittelli in Dave Lambert's 224 Cornelia Street apartment, December 5, 1959. Lamantia's *Narcotica* and *Ekstasis* were both published in 1959.

Above: David Meltzer in the Discovery Book Shop on Columbus Avenue, June 5, 1960.

Right page: Poets Robert Bly (left) and Kenneth Rexroth at a New York University lecture, April 22, 1960. Rexroth broke with the Beats when he thought they became too commercial.

poem for a girl i booted

shall i say that to me

you were as lasting as a cloud

you who are so catlike

with your eyes of agate

with your breasts of fruit

webbed with your hair of silk

shall i tell of your kiss

the fever of your lips

the invitation to destroy myself

to be devoured without regrets

in the flame of your thighs

you are the sea

in all its moods & colors

the times of tranquillity

the fury of your sudden storms

who lured me as greeks were lured

who fondled me with soft waves

then threw me against the rocks

what shall i say of you

i who have the sunrage in my eyes

the moons madness in my mind

the manspike for your frame of flowers

what shall i say

having promised you a poem

even so

what could be more a poem

than the sight of you

high over the city & harbor

with the wind fingering your hair

indeed what could be

for cristina ibiza 58

238

streetandparkscenes

Greenwich Village's identity as America's Bohemia dates back to the midnineteenth century, when writers like Edgar Allan Poe, Walt Whitman, and Horace Greeley came to live in its once-fashionable townhouses. Abandoned by wealthy families who were moving uptown to newer neighborhoods, their brownstone-fronted mansions were divided into flats and studios. Even the stables were converted into little houses. Cheap rents were the chief attraction, but the Village's low-scale buildings and little lanes added a romantic atmosphere not lost on the writers and artists who moved here.

Over the decades, rents in the Village have soared, but the area has remained a magnet for writers and painters. In the mid-1950s, it was a natural gathering place for the Beats, who read poetry in Village coffee houses, although many lived further east, settling in the less-pricey tenements of the East Village.

Sunday afternoon was the time to stroll to Washington Square Park, where an eclectic crowd of mothers, fathers, and babies; artists and intellectuals; bankers and Buddhists; poets and musicians all congregated. Entertainment was free: There might be an impromptu folk concert, or a Beat poet might be inspired to open his notebook and read his latest work. In the park or on the street, a stroll in the Village was bound to result in a serendipitous meeting with a kindred soul.

Looking north on MacDougal Street, from Bleecker, September 27, 1959. Most of the old Beat haunts, like the San Remo Cafe (left foreground), are long since gone.

Bob Lubin and William Morris in front of 22 Greenwich Avenue, the first *Village Voice* office, August 21, 1959. The cobble-stones are now covered over with asphalt.

Louisiana poet Dick Woods on MacDougal Street, August 2, 1959. He is wearing a typically eclectic Beat costume: beret, dragon earrings, dark sunglasses, a necklace with twin Congo figures, Mexican peasant shirt, Peruvian vest, an Indian sash, plus sandals (not pictured).

Beat poets from Washington, D.C., making the MacDougal Street scene, July 18, 1959. Left to right: Dick Munske, Pete Coonley, Bill Jackson, Dick Dabney, and Bob Collins (in foreground).

Poet Howard Hart and friend Cindy Lee (nee Amelia Maria-Theresa Laracuen) on Fifth Avenue and 21st Street, September 4, 1959.

"Angel," a Brooklyn College student, was selected Miss Beatnik of 1959. She is posing on MacDougal Street, in front of the 1931 Chevrolet Independence wood-wheeled roadster owned by radio monologuist Jean Shepherd. Miss Beatnik is now a psychoanalyst, mother of three, and a grandmother.

Ambrose Hollingworth on MacDougal Street, June 21, 1959. His vest is held together with a safety pin. Fringed leather jackets became popular with sixties rock stars. His friend, Louise, has bells around her neck and carries a hand-carved walking stick from Nigeria.

Poet Tuli Kupferberg, center, in front of the Gaslight Cafe, 116 MacDougal Street, March 8, 1959. Behind him are Sheila Bryant and, left, Sylvia Topp.

William Morris reading poetry, July 26, 1959, in Washington Square Park while his friend, Malcolm Soule, looks on. The week before, police had arrested Morris on a disorderly conduct charge for attracting a crowd.

Harry Proach of the Living Theatre takes the message into Washington Square Park, July 19, 1959. He played in Brecht's *In the Jungle of Cities*, Jackson Mac Low's *The Marrying Maiden*, and Jack Gelber's *The Connection*.

Village Voice publisher Edwin Fancher, editor Daniel Wolf, associate editor Jerry Tallmer, and columnist Louise Tallmer near the *Voice*'s first office, 22 Greenwich Avenue, on August 20, 1959.

Poet Bruce Fearing in front of 180 MacDougal Street, October 9, 1959.

Writer and filmmaker Mark Sufrin, actor and director Stanley Phillips, and critic and author Anatole Broyard in Washington Square Park, September 28, 1958.

Fred W. McDarrah, Norman Mailer, Harold L. (Doc) Humes, and Marvin Frank in Washington Square Park, May 15, 1960.

Journalists Nat Hentoff (left) and Gilbert Millstein in Washington Square Park, April 8, 1960.

Right page: Writer Djuna Barnes shopping on Greenwich Avenue, August 14, 1959. The author of *Nightwood* lived nearby on Patchin Place.

Joyce and Ted Joans and their four children in Washington Square Park, June 7, 1959.

Top: Dennis Hopper (left) and Terry Southern at the Chelsea Hotel, September 30, 1971.

Bottom: Gregory Corso, Allen Ginsberg, William Burroughs, and Maretta Green after visiting Timothy Leary's L.S.D. Center, Hudson and Perry Sts., N.Y., February 15, 1967.

The Physical World

Regimented by the sun, the leaves, my own
breathing, the colors of Birdie's dress,
another woman's voice. I mean
I am pinned here; inert, the Brontosorous(a
big, but peaceable vegetarian) Immobile
as the sinister museum walls. In This Time .
In all these things concept of it.

It is"impossible"(meaning that word
like those jocular ladies with
twittery hats, "My deah, he's impossible!")
Loving something you cannot name!

Think of the chaos, out among those islands
the sea twisting & unlettered, THE ROAR.
You said, "Oh, I love being like this! I love it!"
And we both, as the gulls in low spirals out of
the sun, screaming over THE ROAR, knew
what you meant... But
Nothing roars here.

A portion of me unable to control itself
creeps out, hovering above all these twisted
sad immobile meaningless gray gray gray gray
gray gray gray gray gray gray gray gray gray
gray gray gray gray gray gray gray gray gray

The world, my life, all your beauties, your hair,
even your hair, the afternoon (Autumn trailing
after me, again, I age, each new sun means I age,
leant further away from what has meaning for me.
"I will never be a boy again." So much death in that;
and now to sit here listening, No..not even being able
to listen#to this electric clock, a mere artifact, telling me
I am going to die. And the jungle of memory, hot and sinister,
strange beasts, their cries in my head, sitting inert, unable
to raise my eyes in protest. (NO, that is meaningless, Unable
to inhale the warm fall air, without seeing it structured around me
like a room, a gray room, where I sit & dream of myself & you
& the sea we will never be so close to again.

                                              -LeRoi Jones
                                               402 W.20th St.
                                               NYC 11,

the wilentzes and the 8th street bookshop

Ted Wilentz opened the 8th Street Bookshop in partnership with his brother, Eli, shortly after World War II. They bought a small Womrath's chain bookstore on MacDougal Street in 1947. In addition to selling books, the store also had a lending library, sold greeting cards, stationery, and small gift items. The Wilentzes changed the store, and it became a purely literary shop. Writers and readers responded strongly, and the store was a success. It became a center for many writers of the 1950s, including Corso, Ginsberg, and LeRoi Jones; Hettie Jones worked at the store for a while. Ted and his family lived in an apartment above the store, and there he threw his informal book parties, which were the closest thing to a literary salon in the Greenwich Village of the 1950s.

Their publishing house, Corinth Books, grew out of their success with the bookshop. The first publication, in 1959, was a fifty-cent guidebook to the Village that included McDarrah photographs. An eclectic variety of books followed, including work by Frank O'Hara, Gary Snyder, Charles Olson, Diane diPrima, Ted Joans, Delmore Schwartz, Dan Wakefield, and LeRoi Jones. Corinth published the anthology *The Beat Scene*, which Ted Wilentz kept in print for a remarkable twenty-three years.

The Wilentz brothers split up in 1968; Ted and his wife Joan continued Corinth Press as co-editors and co-publishers, and Eli took over sole management of the store. It later moved across 8th Street where a disastrous fire eventually led to its close.

Eli and Ted Wilentz's 8th Street Bookshop, May 16, 1959.

Allen Ginsberg, Donald Allen, and Lawrence Ferlinghetti.

Dancer Cynthia Fancher, her brother Ed, David McReynolds, Marsha Berman, and Allen Ginsberg.

Artist Edward Clark (rear), William Morris (in center with cigarette), Howard Smith (beard), A. B. Spellman, Jim Spicer of the Living Theatre (rear, white shirt), and Richard Howard (right).

Top: Poet A. B. Spellman (back to camera), Bonnie Bremser, Ray Bremser, and Marion Zazeela talking about the Bremsers' new baby at a Wilentz party, September 17, 1960.

Bottom: Ted Wilentz and Allen Ginsberg at a poetry party, September 17, 1960.

Dancer Remy Charlip and editor Hettie Jones at a Wilentz party, September 17, 1960.

May Swenson

The Shape of Death

What does love look like? We know the shape of death:
death is a cloud, immense and awesome.
At first a lid is lifted from the eye of light;
there is a clap of sound; a white blossom
belches from the jaw of fright;
a pillared cloud churns from white to gray,
like a monstrous brain that bursts and burns,
then turns sickly black, spilling and spewing away,
filling the whole sky with ashes of dread.
Thickly it wraps, between the clean seas and the moon,
the earth's green head. Trapped in its cocoon,
its choking breath, we know the shape of death.
Death is a cloud.

What does love look like? Is it a particle, a star,
invisible entirely, beyond the microscope and Palomar;
a dimension unimagined, past the stretch of hope?
Is it a climate far and fair, that we shall never dare
discover? What is its color, and its alchemy?
Is it a jewel in the earth; can it be dug?
or dredged from the sea? Can it be bought?
Can it be sown and harvested? Is it a shy beast to be caught?

Death is a cloud, immense, a clap of sound.
Love is little, and not loud.
It nests within each cell, and it
cannot be split.
It is a ray, a seed, a note, a word,
a secret motion of our air and blood.
Love is not alien; it is near;
it is our very skin,
a sheathe that keeps us pure of fear.

laststop:lowell

When Kerouac's first book, *The Town and the City*, was published in 1950, he returned to Lowell, Massachusetts, the factory town where he was born in 1922 and had spent his boyhood, for an autographing party in a department store. But the book was not selling well, and few beyond his old friends showed up, thus making the event little more than a nostalgic reunion. After Kerouac died, on October 21, 1969, it seemed unlikely that Lowell would find any reason to claim him as a native son. But in the following two decades, more and more literary pilgrims made their way to Lowell to visit the sites that figured in his novels, as well as his grave in Edson Cemetery. With Lowell's textile factories no longer providing jobs, Kerouac's value to the town's economy as a tourist attraction became obvious. And so the city council voted, in 1986, to put up a commemorative sculpture to Kerouac, even though there were arguments that "the action would glorify the abuse of both alcohol and drugs."

The memorial was completed in 1988, and is an awe-inspiring sight, reminiscent of the prehistoric slabs of Stonehenge. There are eight triangular marble columns, arranged in a plaza in the Eastern Canal Park at French and Bridge streets. Each of the polished reddish-brown marble slabs is incised with excerpts from his novels: *The Town and the City*, *On the Road*, *Mexico City Blues*, *Book of Dreams*, and *Doctor Sax*. Guided tours include the Kerouac memorial, as well as sites such as the Ste. Jeanne d'Arc Church, Bootts Mills, Lowell High School clock, and the Moody Street Bridge, as well as Kerouac's grave site.

Excerpts from Kerouac's books are sandblasted into the Carnelian marble of the commemorative monument in one-acre Eastern Canal Park in Lowell's historic district.

Jack Kerouac's simple gravestone in Edson Cemetery on Gorham Street attracts a host of literary pilgrims who pay their respects with everything from flowers to beer cans.

Jack Kerouac, 1922–1969.

bibliography

Allen, Donald M., ed. *The New American Poetry: 1945–1960*. New York: Grove, 1960.

Allen, Donald M., and Warren Tallman, eds. *Poetics of the New American Poetry*. New York: Grove, 1974.

Amram, David. *Vibrations: The Adventures and Musical Times of David Amram*. New York: Macmillan, 1968.

Anderson, Elliot, ed. *TriQuarterly 43, the Little Magazine in America: A Modern Documentary History*. Evanston, Ill.: Northwestern University, 1978.

Ball, Gordon, ed. *Allen Verbatim: Lectures on Poetry, Politics, Consciousness*. New York: McGraw-Hill, 1974.

Bartlett, Lee, ed. *The Beats: Essays in Criticism*. Jefferson, N. Car.: McFarland, 1981.

Beaulieu, Victor-Levy. *Jack Kerouac: A Chicken-Essay*. Toronto: Coach House Press, 1975.

Berkson, Bill, and Joe LeSueur. *Homage to Frank O'Hara*. Bolinas, Calif.: Big Sky, 1978.

Berthoff, Warner. *A Literature Without Qualities: American Writing Since 1945*. Berkeley: University of California Press, 1979.

Breslin, Paul. *The Psycho-Political Muse: American Poetry Since the Fifties*. Chicago: University of Chicago Press, 1987.

Cassady, Carolyn. *Heart Beat: My Life with Jack and Neal*. Berkeley: Creative Arts Book Co., 1976.

———. *Off the Road: My Years with Cassady, Kerouac and Ginsberg*. New York: William Morrow and Co., 1990.

Charters, Ann. *Jack Kerouac: Selected Letters 1940–1956*. Viking Penguin, 1995.

———. *The Portable Beat Reader*. New York: Viking Penguin, 1992.

———. *Beats and Company*. New York: Doubleday, 1986.

Charters, Ann, ed. *The Beats: Literary Bohemians in Postwar America*. Vol. 16, Parts 1 and 2 of <I>Dictionary of Literary Biography<I>. Detroit: Gale Research Co., 1983.

Charters, Ann. *Kerouac, a Biography*. San Francisco: Straight Arrow Books, 1973.

———. *Scenes Along the Road: Photographs of the Desolation Angels, 1944–1960*. New York: Portents/Gotham Book Mart, 1970.

Charters, Samuel. *Some Poems/Poets: Studies in American Underground Poetry Since 1945*. Berkeley, Calif.: Oyez, 1971.

Clark, Tom. *Jack Kerouac*. San Diego: Harcourt Brace Jovanovich, 1984.

Cook, Bruce. *The Beat Generation*. New York: Scribners, 1971.

Cook, Ralph T. *The City Lights Pocket Poets Series: A Descriptive Bibliography*. La Jolla, Calif.: McGilvery/Atticus Books, 1982.

Davidson, Michael. *The San Francissco Renaissance: Poetrics and Community at Mid-Century*. New York: Cambridge University Press, 1989.

DiPrima, Diane. *Memoirs of a Beatnik*. New York: Olympia, 1969.

Ehrlich, J. W., ed. *Howl of the Censor: The Four Letter Word on Trial*. San Carlos, Calif.: Nourse, 1961.

Fass, Ekbert. *Towards a New American Poetrics: Essays and Interviews*. Santa Barbara, Calif.: Black Sparrow Press, 1979.

Feied, Frederick. *No Pie in the Sky: The Hobo as American Cultural Hero in the Works of Jack London, John Dos Passos, and Jack Kerouac*. New York: Citadel, 1964.

Feldman, Gene, and Max Gartenberg, eds. *The Beat Generation and the Angry Young Men*. New York: Citadel, 1958.

Felver, Christopher. *The Poet Exposed*. New York: Alfred Van Der Marck Editions, 1986.

Ferlinghetti, Lawrence, ed. *Beatitude Anthology*. San Francisco: City Lights Books, 1960.

Ferlinghetti, Lawrence, and Nancy J. Peters. *Literary San Francisco: A Pictorial History from Its Beginnings to the Present*. San Francisco: City Lights Books/Harper & Row, 1980.

French, Warren. *The San Francisco Poetry*

Renaissance, 1955–1960. Boston: Twayne Publishers, 1991.

Gifford, Barry. *Kerouac's Town*. Photographs by Marshall Clements. Berkeley, Calif.: Creative Arts Book Co., 1977.

Gifford, Barry, and Lawrence Lee, eds. *Jack's Book*. New York: St. Martin's, 1978.

Ginsberg, Allen. *Snapshot Poetics*. San Francisco: Chronicle Books, 1993.

———. *Howl: Original Draft Facsimile, Transcript and Variant Versions*. Edited by Barry Miles. New York: Harper & Row, 1986.

———. *The Visions of the Great Remember*. Amherst, Mass.: Mulch Press, 1974.

Gold, Herbert. *Bohemia: Where Art, Angst, Love, and Strong Coffee Meet*. New York: Simon & Schuster, 1993.

Gooch, Brad. *The Life and Times of Frank O'Hara*. New York: Alfred A. Knopf, 1993.

Goodman, Michael Barry. *Contemporary Literary Censorship: The Case History of Naked Lunch*. Metuchen, N. J. and London: Scarecrow Press, 1981.

Gruen, John, with photographs by Fred W. McDarrah. *The New Bohemia*. New York: Shorecrest, Inc., 1966; reprinted Chicago: a cappella books, 1990.

Harris, Oliver. *The Letters of William S. Burroughs: 1945–1959*. New York: Viking Penguin, 1993.

Hipkiss, Robert A. *Jack Kerouac: Prophet of the New Romanticism*. Lawrence: Regents Press of Kansas, 1976.

Hoffman, Frederick J. *Marginal Manners: The Variants of Bohemia*. Evanston, Ill.: Row, Peterson, 1962.

Holmes, John Clellon. *Nothing More to Declare*. New York: Dutton, 1967.

Honan, Park. *The Beats*. London: J. M. Dent & Sons, Ltd., 1987.

Hornick, Lita. *The Green Fuse: A Memoir*. New York: Giorno Poetry Systems, 1989.

Howard, Richard. *Alone with America: Essays on the Art of Poetry in the United States Since 1950*. New York: Atheneum, 1980.

Huebel, Harry Russell. *Jack Kerouac*. Boise, Idaho: Boise State University, 1979.

Hunt, Tim. *Kerouac's Crooked Road: Development of a Fiction*. Hamden, Conn.: Archon Books, 1981.

Hyde, Lewis, ed. *On the Poetry of Allen Ginsberg*. Ann Arbor, Mich.: University of Michigan Press, 1984.

Johnson, Joyce. *Minor Characters*. Boston: Houghton Mifflin, 1983.

Jones, Hettie. *How I Became Hettie Jones*. New York: E. P. Dutton, 1990.

Jones, LeRoi, ed. *The Moderns: An Anthology of New Writing in America*. New York: Corinth, 1963.

Knight, Arthur, and Kit Knight. *Kerouac and the Beats*. New York: Paragon House, 1988.

———. *The Beat Vision*. New York: Paragon House, 1987.

———. *Beat Angels*. California, Pa.: Unspeakable Visions of the Individual, 1982.

———. *The Beat Road*. California, Pa.: Unspeakable Visions of the Individual, 1982.

———. *The Beat Journey*. California, Pa.: Unspeakable Visions of the Individual, 1978.

———. *The Beat Diary*. California, Pa.: Unspeakable Visions of the Individual, 1977.

———. *The Beat Book*. California, Pa.: Unspeakable Visions of the Individual, 1974.

Kostelanetz, Richard. *Master Minds*. New York: Macmillan, 1969.

———. *Twenties in the Sixties*. Westport, Conn.: Greenwood Press, 1979.

Kramer, Jane. *Allen Ginsberg in America*. New York: Random House, 1968.

Krim, Seymour, ed. *The Beats*. New York: Fawcett, 1960.

Lepper, Gary M. *A Bibliographical Introduction to Seventy-Five Modern American Authors*. Berkeley: Serendipity Books, 1976.

Lipton, Lawrence. *The Holy Barbarians*. New York: Messner, 1959.

McDarrah, Fred W. *Kerouac & Friends: A Beat Generation Album*. New York: William Morrow, 1985.

———. *The Beat Scene*. Edited by Eli Wilentz. New York: Corinth Books, 1960.

McDarrah, Fred W., and Patrick J. McDarrah. *The Greenwich Village Guide*. Chicago: a cappella books/Chicago Review Press, 1992.

McNally, Dennis. *Desolate Angel: Jack Kerouac, the Beats & America*. New York: Random House, 1979.

Meltzer, David, ed. *The San Francisco Beats*. New York: Ballantine, 1971.

Miles, Barry. *William Burroughs El Hombre Invisible: A Portrait*. New York: Hyperion, 1993.

———. *Ginsberg, A Biography.* New York: Simon & Schuster, 1989.

Milewski, Robert J. *Jack Kerouac: An Annotated Bibliography of Secondary Sources, 1944–1979.* Metuchen, N. J.: Scarecrow Press, 1981.

Moore, Harry T., ed. *Contemporary American Novelists.* Carbondale, Ill.: Southern Illinois University Press, 1964.

Morgan, Bill, and Bob Rosenthal. *Best Minds: A Tribute to Allen Ginsberg.* New York: Lospecchio Press, 1986.

Morgan, Ted. *Literary Outlaw: The Life and Times of William S. Burroughs.* New York: Henry Holt, 1988.

Nicosia, Gerald. *Memory Babe: A Critical Biography of Jack Kerouac.* New York: Grove, 1983.

Norse, Harold. *Memories of a Bastard Angel.* New York: William Morrow, 1989.

———. *Beat Hotel.* San Diego: Atticus, 1983.

Nowinski, Ira. *Cafe Society: Photographs and Poetry from San Francisco's North Beach.* San Francisco: Seefood Studios–Two Continents Publishing, 1978.

Ossman, David. *The Sullen Art: Interviews by David Ossman with Modern American Poets.* New York: Corinth Books, 1963.

Parkinson Thomas, ed. *A Casebook on the Beat.* New York: Thomas Y. Crowell, 1961.

Perloff, Marjorie. *Frank O'Hara, Poet Among Painters.* Austin, Texas: University of Texas, 1977.

Plummer, William. *The Holy Goof.* Englewood Cliffs, N. J.: Prentice-Hall, 1981.

Rexroth, Kenneth. *American Poetry in the Twentieth Century.* New York: Herder & Herder, 1971.

Rigney, Francis J., and L. Douglas Smith. *The Real Bohemia: A Sociological and Psychological Study of the Beats.* New York: Basic Books, 1961.

Sanders, Ed. *Tales of Beatnik Glory.* New York: Stonehill, 1975.

Saroyan, Aram. *Genesis Angels: The Saga of Lew Welch and the Beat Generation.* New York: Morrow, 1979.

Seaver, Richard, Terry Southern, and Alexander Trocchi, eds. *Writers in Revolt.* New York: Frederick Fell, 1963.

Skerl, Jennie. *William S. Burroughs.* Boston: Twayne, 1985.

Skerl, Jennie, and Robin Lydenberg. *William S. Burroughs: At the Front.* Carbondale, Ill.: Southern Illinois University Press, 1991.

Sukenick, Ronald. *Down and In: Life in the Underground.* New York: Collier Books, 1987.

Tonkinson, Carole. *Big Sky Mind: Buddhism and the Beat Generation.* New York: Riverhead Books, 1995.

Tytell, John. *The Living Theatre: Art, Exile, and Outrage.* New York: Grove Press, 1995.

———. *Naked Angels: The Lives and Literature of the Beat Generation.* New York: McGraw-Hill, 1977.

Wakefield, Dan. *New York in the Fifties.* Boston: Houghton Mifflin/Seymour Lawrence, 1992.

Waldmeir, Joseph J., ed. *Recent American Fiction: Some Critical Views.* Boston: Houghton Mifflin, 1963.

Watson, Steven. *The Birth of the Beat Generation: Visionaries, Rebels, and Hipsters, 1944–1960.* New York: Pantheon, 1995.

Weinreich, Regina. *The Spontaneous Poetics of Jack Kerouac.* Carbondale, Ill.: Southern Illinois University Press, 1987.

Welch, Lew. *I Remain: The Letters of Lew Welch & the Correspondence of his Friends.* Vol. 1, 1949–1960; Vol. 2, 1960–1971. Edited by Don Allen. Bolinas, Calif.: Grey Fox Press, 1980.

Wolf, Daniel, and Edwin Fancher. *The Village Voice Reader.* New York: Doubleday, 1962.

biographical sketches

Daisy Aldan, publisher, editor, translator, edited the celebrated anthology series *A New Folder*, which published poets and painters of the New York School. She was nominated for a Pulitzer prize in poetry for *Between High Tides*, and runs New Folder Editions Press.

Donald M. Allen compiled the anthology *The New American Poetry: 1945—1960* (Grove Press, 1960), launching the careers of many American postmodern writers and poets. Allen was also first coeditor of the original *Evergreen Review*. He lives in San Francisco and is editor and publisher of Grey Fox Press.

Rick Allmen, who came from the Lower East Side, started the Cafe Bizarre with $100. It became one of the most colorful coffee houses in Greenwich Village in the late 1950s. Allmen was on the committee that battled City Hall and the police department to permit poetry readings in coffee houses. In 1983 the entire block where the cafe stood was demolished.

David Amram is a composer, conductor, musician, and actor who played in the famous film *Pull My Daisy*. In March 1957, Amram was among the first musicians to combine jazz with Beat poetry in performances at Circle in the Square and the Brata Gallery. He continues to perform and compose today in a variety of jazz and world-music influenced styles.

Alfred G. Aronowitz was the first print journalist to write, in 1959 in the *New York Post*, seriously about the Beat Generation as a literary movement. His latest work is *Blacklisted Masterpieces of Al Aronowitz*.

John Ashbery, born in Rochester, N.Y., is a noted New York School poet and critic. His poetry collection *Self-Portrait in a Convex Mirror* (1976) won both the National Book Award and Pulitzer prize. He was formerly editor of *Art News*.

W. H. (Wystan Hugh) Auden lived in the East Village in the Beat era and occasionally read his poetry at academic venues like the New School. Ranked among the major literary figures of the 20th century, British-born Auden moved to the United States in 1939 and became a citizen in 1946. He died in 1973.

Edward Avedisian, born, like Kerouac, in Lowell, Mass., is a painter and sculptor. Avedisian studied at the Boston Museum School of Art. His work is in major museum collections throughout the country. Avedisian now lives in Hudson, N.Y.

James Baldwin, novelist, essayist, and playwright, became one of this country's most respected and successful writers. The eldest of nine children, he grew up in Harlem. He moved to Paris in 1948 and lived as an expatriate for two decades. He died in 1987 in St. Paul de Vence.

Djuna Barnes gained fame from her literary experiments: *The Book of Repulsive Women* and later her extraordinary 1936 novel *Nightwood* were among the first books to express a lesbian sensibility. In her later years, she was a familiar figure on Greenwich Village streets. She died June 19, 1982, at the age of 90.

Robert Beauchamp, a figurative painter known for his colorful, expressionistic style, was born in Denver and studied with Hans Hoffman in Provincetown, Mass. Beauchamp's subjects included exotic birds, monkeys, wild horses, and other beasts. His first exhibit was at the Tanager Gallery in 1953; he died in 1995.

Julian Beck, together with his wife, Judith Malina, began the Living Theatre in 1951. The theater became a center for poetry readings, dramatic performances, and concerts, until the building was seized by the IRS in 1963. The company went into exile abroad, although they returned triumphantly to a new theater in New York in the late 1960s; it is still in existence today. Beck died in 1985.

Bill Berkson is a poet and art critic, and was the editor and publisher of *Big Sky* magazine. With playwright and novelist Joe LeSueur, he edited *Homage to Frank O'Hara*. Berkson lives in Solinas, Calif.

Paul Blackburn was born in Vermont, and was a Fulbright scholar as well as a Guggenheim fellow. Poet, translator, and contributing editor of *Black Mountain Review*, Blackburn lived in Spain in the mid-1950s. *The Dissolving Fabric*, his first book, was published in 1955; altogether he wrote nineteen books. He died in 1971 at the age of 41. His *Collected Poems*, edited by Edie Jarolim, appeared in 1989.

Lester Blackiston, born in Texas, began his association with the Beat movement in Provincetown. When he lived in New York, Blackiston was among the group that organized the meetings to bury the Beat Generation. He now lives in Richmond, Va., where he is a charter boat captain.

Ronald Bladen, a second-generation New York School sculptor, was born in Vancouver, British Columbia. His abstract, minimalist sculptures have been exhibited at the Whitney and Guggenheim museums in New York, and he is represented in many other museum collections nationwide. Bladen, who was a recipient of National Endowment and Guggenheim Foundation awards, died in 1988.

Tamara Bliss, born in Moscow and educated in Canada and at Barnard College, is a composer, concert pianist, and teacher at the New School. She wrote the music for three off-Broadway plays as well as the score for the noted de Kooning documentary film. Bliss is currently musical director of the Downtown Theatre Project.

Roberts Blossom was a minor Beat poet and an off-Broadway actor. After appearing off-Broadway, Blossom played on Broadway in *Ballad of the Sad Cafe* and *The Cherry Orchard*. He moved on to Hollywood and a film career, with roles in major motion pictures such as *Home Alone*, *The Great Gatsby*, and *Close Encounters*.

Robert Bly achieved popular fame with his *Iron John: A Book about Men* (1990), which became an icon of the men's movement. Born in Minnesota to a farm family, he has been an important influence on contemporary poets as a poet and critic himself, as translator of Neruda and Rilke, and as editor of the magazine series *The Fifties*, *The Sixties*, *The Seventies*, etc.

Ray Bremser was born in Jersey City, N.J., in 1934, participated in armed robbery, and did six years at Bordentown Reformatory, where he wrote his first poems at the age of 18. He later married Bonnie Frazer, and, again in trouble with the law, fled to Mexico. Much of Bremser's writing—*Angel*, *Drive Suite*, *Blowing Mouth/The Jazz Poems 1958–1970*—was done at Rahway State Prison. Plagued by drugs and alcohol, Bremser eventually moved to Utica, N. Y. He has published five books of poetry.

Anatole Broyard, born in New Orleans, was a book critic, columnist, and editor for the *New York Times*. In his final book, *Kafka Was the Rage: A Greenwich Village Memoir* (1993), published posthumously, Broyard describes his youthful days meeting all the Village luminaries.

William S. Burroughs, legendary Beat figure born in St. Louis in 1914, was the grandson of the inventor of the Burroughs adding machine. He met Kerouac and Ginsberg in 1944. He worked as a private detective, exterminator, and bartender. Burroughs chose drugs as a way of life and settled in Tangiers in 1953, the year he published *Junkie: Confessions of an Unredeemed Drug Addict*. His knowledge of addicts, criminals, and sexual deviates was the basis of his famous 1959 book *Naked Lunch*. In Kerouac's novels Burroughs is identified as Will Dennison, Will Hubbard, and Frank Carmody, and in *On the Road* as Old Bull Lee. Burroughs continues to write both fiction and nonfiction works.

Rick Carrier, although not a member of the Beat movement, was a notable figure on the Provincetown and Village literary scenes. He was a documentary filmmaker and author with his wife, Barbara, of *Dive*, about deep sea diving.

Paul Carroll, one of the patriarchs of the Chicago poetry world, came from a banking and real-estate family, attended the University of Chicago, and was editor of *Big Table*. A poet and literary critic, Carroll is professor of English at the University of Illinois and founding president of the Poetry Center of the Art Institute of Chicago.

Neal Cassady, legendary hero in the Beat movement, was born in Salt Lake City to a life of hardship, married three times, was immortalized as Dean Moriarty in Kerouac's *On the Road*, and died in Mexico in 1968, presumably of drugs and alcohol, four days before his 43rd birthday. His body was found beside the railway tracks in San Miguel de Allende. His autobiography, *The First Third*, was published in 1971 by City Lights Books.

Remy Charlip is a choreographer, dancer, painter, designer, teacher, and author of books and songs. His twenty-six picture books have won many awards worldwide. He has been choreographing and dancing since 1949. He lives in San Francisco.

Paddy Chayefsky, a native New Yorker and a City College graduate, was best-known for his 1955 television and film drama *Marty* and his Oscar-winning film *Network*. He died in 1981.

Alfred Chester was born in Brooklyn in 1928. X-ray treatments for a childhood disease caused him to lose his hair, even his eyelashes and eyebrows. His baldness made him feel like a freak, and his feelings of alienation would haunt him throughout his life. He was an expatriate for most of his adult life. He wrote novels, short stories, essays, and criticism. He was twice a Guggenheim fellow. In the early 1970s, he went to Jerusalem, where he died at age 42 of an overdose.

Robert Cordier, poet, playwright, and stage and film director, was born in Belgium, came to New York in the 1950s, and worked as an off-Broadway director. His feature film about the New York rock scene, *Injun Fender*, won several major awards. He now lives in Paris, where his play, *Hattie's Song in Babylone So Cold*, won France's Ministry of Culture award.

Gregory Corso, who was born in Greenwich Village, was interested in writing even before he became an inmate in the state prison in Dannemora, N.Y., where he read all the books in the library. Corso's best-known poem, "Bomb," was published in 1958 by City Lights. Corso, with Ginsberg and Orlovsky, lived in Paris at the notorious Beatnik Hotel at 9 rue Git-le-Coeur until 1961. The anxiety of waiting for money at American Express offices apparently led to the title of his only novel, *American Express*, a work of surrealist episodes. He continues to write and lecture.

Jimmy Cuchiara made his mark on the New York art scene in the late 1940s, by creating "The School for Pure Plastic Painting," on 10th Street. He was a founding member of the Phoenix Gallery in 1958. In 1970, Cuchiara ran for New York State Senate but lost. He now divides his time between Miami Beach—where he initially worked as a courtroom illustrator and now is an art critic for the *Miami Sun Post*—and the Virgin Islands, where he owns several stores.

Paul Cummings was curator of drawings at the Whitney Museum and is now president of the Drawing Society. He is the author of several books on contemporary graphic art.

Dick Dabney was raised in Virginia. During the Beat era, he wrote for the *Washington Post Weekly*, an underground paper. Later he was an op-ed page columnist for the *Washington Post* and contributor to *Washingtonian* magazine. His best-known work is *A Good Man: The Life of Sam J. Erwin*. In November 1981, Dabney died at the age of 48.

Richard Davidson was born in Chicago and came to New York in 1954. He gave numerous poetry readings at the Gaslight and other coffee houses. His work has appeared in many literary magazines, and he is the author of four poetry books.

Fielding Dawson was born in New York, grew up in Missouri, and attended Black Mountain College. An artist and illustrator as well as poet and author, his paintings, drawings, and collages have been exhibited widely. He was contributing artist for Daisy Aldan's *New Folder* and Gilbert Sorrentino's *Neon*, and author of a memoir of Franz Kline.

Diane di Prima published her first book, *This Kind of Bird Flies Backwards*, with LeRoi Jones's Totem Press in 1958. She edited the literary magazine *Floating Bear* with LeRoi Jones. She dedicated *Dinners & Nightmares*, a book of prose sketches (1961) to her "pads and the people who shared them." Di Prima has more than fifteen books to her credit, including *Memories of a Beatnik*. Many of her plays were performed by the Living Theatre. Born in Brooklyn, she has been living and teaching in California.

Lucia Dlugoszewski, an American composer, moved to New York to study with Edgard Varèse in the early 1950s. Much of her music, influenced by Asian poetry and scientific philosophy, was commissioned for the Erick Hawkins Dance Company. Among her musical innovations are the "timbre piano" and families of unusual percussion instruments, such as tangent rattles and ladder harps.

Kirby Doyle's best-known work, *Happiness Bastard*, written in 1958, is autobiographic, dealing with his struggle to survive out of jail, despite poverty, drug addiction, and unhappy love affairs. A well-known poet through the 1950s, his first collection of verse, *Sapphobones*, did not appear until 1966. Doyle stopped writing for over ten years and lived alone in the wilderness in California before returning to North Beach in 1982 to finish his epic trilogy, *Pre-American Ode*. Green Light Press in San Francisco brought out his *Collected Works* in 1984.

Robert Duncan edited the *Experimental Review*, one of the first magazines to publish postwar American poetry. He has written over thirty-five books since the late 1940s and was at the heart of literary activity in the San Francisco Bay area for four decades. Duncan broke ground in 1944 by publishing a controversial essay, "The Homosexual in Society," on a topic then rarely mentioned in public. He died in 1988.

Frederick W. Dupee came east from Chicago to study at Yale, where he became, in his own words, a "dedicated literary man." He became literary editor of *New Masses* in 1936, and later a founder of *Partisan Review*. Dupee was in the English Department of Columbia when he was chosen by the John Dewey Society to chair the 1959 poetry reading by Beat poets that brought Allen Ginsberg in a victorious homecoming back to the school that had dismissed him years before.

Kenward Elmslie, a 1950 Harvard graduate, is a librettist, poet, playwright, and novelist who now lives in Vermont. He was one of the inner circle of Frank O'Hara's New York School.

Edwin Fancher, a practicing psychologist, was cofounder with Daniel Wolf and Norman Mailer of the *Village Voice*, and its publisher for the first nineteen years.

Bruce Fearing, son of the well-known Chicago novelist Kenneth Fearing, graduated from Harvard and at one time was a science writer. Later, his cryptic poetry appeared in Beat literary magazines. He moved to Seattle and sent friends photocopied letters filled with Beat humor, referring to himself as "bruce goose," "son of mother goose," and to Gregory Corso as "Gregory Kerchoo."

Lawrence Ferlinghetti, born in Yonkers, N.Y., attended Columbia and the University of Paris, where he received his doctorate. He moved to San Francisco and started City Lights Books and cofounded the bookstore with Peter D. Martin in the early 1950s. Ferlinghetti published Ginsberg's *Howl*, Corso's *Gasoline*, and Kerouac's *Book of Dreams*, and later books by Charles Bukowski and Sam Shepard. Ferlinghetti's own best-seller, *A Coney Island of the Mind*, has over a million copies in print. His "Horn on Howl," an account of the landmark "Howl" obscenity case, was published in *Evergreen Review* in 1957. (Clayton Horn was the judge in the case.)

Jackie Ferrara, born in Detroit, is a sculptor whose work has ranged from abstract forms to ghostly effigies placed in coffin-like boxes. Her work is in the collections of the Museum of Modern Art and Metropolitan Museum and has been exhibited nationwide. Ferrara has been the recipient of National Endowment for the Arts and Guggenheim awards.

John Ferren was a noted New York School painter who was an active member of The Artist's Club. He lived in East Hampton and was a friend of Pollock, Krasner, and other East End artists. Ferren, who died in 1970, was an associate professor at Queens College, New York.

Edward Field, born in Brooklyn, served in the Air Force in World War II. His first book of poetry, published by Grove Press in 1963, was awarded the Lamont Poetry Prize. He also edited a poetry anthology for Bantam Books and collaborated on a novel, *Village*, published by Avon under the pseudonym Bruce Elliot.

Stanley Fisher was a talented but underrated artist whose paintings, poetry, and writings had a wide underground reputation. Along with his wife, Anita Fay, he edited *Beat Coast East*, an exceptional collection of Beat writings. Fisher died in 1980.

John Fles was managing editor of the *Chicago Review* and contributing editor of *Kulchur*, and has published poetry in all the Beat literary magazines. He edited a collection of pieces by Antonin Artaud, Jean Genet, and Carl Solomon called *The Trembling Lamb*.

Robert Frank began photographing in Switzerland in 1945 and arrived in New York in March 1947. His great success as a still photographer began with his 1959 book, *The Americans*, with a preface by Kerouac. They also collaborated on the landmark Beat film, *Pull My Daisy*, written and narrated by Kerouac. Photographed in coproducer Alfred Leslie's loft, the film starred Ginsberg, Corso, Orlovsky, Larry Rivers, Alice Neel, David Amram, Dick Bellamy, Delphine Seyrig, and Sally Gross. A major retrospective of Frank's work opened in Washington at the National Gallery in 1994. He was also represented in the 1995 Beat show at the Whitney Museum in New York City.

Brenda Frazer, who published under the name Bonnie Bremser, described the difficult first five years of her marriage in her autobiography *Troia: Mexican Memoirs*, when she followed Ray Bremser to Mexico to evade prison in 1960.

William Gaddis was born in New York, and attended Harvard. Although considered a mainstream writer, Gaddis had strong connections with the Beat movement. His highly successful novel, *The Recognitions*, is his best-known work.

Leo Garin, a director, stage manager, designer, and actor who was involved in over fifty theatrical productions, studied with Lee Strasberg and Harold Clurman. A native of Philadelphia, he left school at age 14 and hitchhiked through the United States and Mexico. Among Garin's notable directorial efforts were Jean Genet's *Deathwatch* and LeRoi Jones's *The Slave* and *The Toilet*, both with sets by Larry Rivers.

Sonia Gechtoff, a Philadelphia-born painter, studied at the Philadelphia Museum College of Art. She has shown extensively since the 1960s and her work is in the collections of many major museums. Gechtoff lives in Greenwich Village.

Jack Gelber wrote the Obie-winning play *The Connection*, produced by the Living Theatre. He also wrote several other plays and a novel, *On Ice*. Among the plays he has directed are Arthur Kopit's *Indians* and Robert Coover's *The Kid*, for which Gelber won an Obie.

Allen Ginsberg, born in Newark, N.J., attended Columbia College, and later sailed in the merchant marine. In 1955 he went to San Francisco. His first book, *Howl and Other Poems*, published by City Lights, created a sensation and was the subject of a famous court case for obscenity. He settled in New York's East Village in the late 1950s, where he continues to live. An active poet, peace activist, and spokesperson for over four decades, Ginsberg organized the Naropa Institute and the Jack Kerouac School of Disembodied Poetics in Boulder, Col. Ginsberg has also achieved renown as a photographer, with more than forty years of pictures of friends and scenes from his travels; his photos have been widely displayed, including at the Whitney Museum Beat Generation show in 1995.

Herbert Gold, two years behind Kerouac at Columbia College, frequently criticized the Beats in his articles, which appeared in several national magazines. Gold characterized some of Kerouac's work as a "flood of trivia," but did praise the novel *Big Sur*. Gold's writings include *Fathers*, *The Man Who Was Not with It*, *True Love*, and *Bohemia*. He lives in San Francisco.

Michael Goldberg, an abstract expressionist painter, studied painting at the Art Students League and at Hans Hofmann's school. Goldberg lived and worked on East 10th Street and was represented in the first shows of the New York School in 1951. Goldberg's work is in major museum collections and has been exhibited worldwide.

Paul Goodman was a social critic and writer of criticism, fiction, poetry, and works on urban planning and psychotherapy. He taught at the University of Chicago and Black Mountain College, but was discharged from both institutions because of his bisexuality. His best-known works are *Growing Up Absurd*, *Speaking and Language*, and *Defense of Poetry*. He lived in New York until his death in 1972.

Garry Goodrow, an actor who played the saxophone, was a friend of playwright Jack Gelber, and was recruited for a pivotal role in the Living Theatre's production of *The Connection*. Goodrow was with the company for many years, before moving on to Hollywood stardom.

Robert von Ranke Graves was an English poet, novelist, essayist, and critic, born in London in 1895; his first poetry was published in 1916. A long-time resident of Majorca, Graves was best-known for his historical novel *I, Claudius* (1934) and his famous book on mythology and literary inspiration, *The White Goddess* (1948). He was a frequent visitor to New York in the 1950s and 1960s, and a well-known presence on the poetry scene.

Maretta Greer had just returned from India in 1964 when she came to Allen Ginsberg's apartment, saying she had heard of his interest in Eastern philosophy. Greer became Ginsberg's mantra-chanting girlfriend on and off for years, staying with him when she was not in India. On January 19, 1967, along with Ginsberg, Timothy Leary, and Gary Snyder, she chanted at the Human Be-In at Golden Gate Park in San Francisco.

Barbara Guest was born in North Carolina and raised in California. She came to New York, where she was associated with the poets and painters of the New York School. She has published twelve volumes of poetry and a novel, *Seeking Air*, collaborated with painters on lithographs and paintings, and written a biography of the poet H. D. Her *Selected Poems* was published in 1995. Guest lives in Berkeley, Calif.

Howard Hart, jazz drummer and free-spirited Catholic poet, shared an apartment with Kerouac and Philip Lamantia in the same building where poet Jack Micheline lived on the Lower East Side. Hart, Kerouac, and David Amram gave the first poetry-and-jazz readings in New York at the Brata Gallery and at the Circle in the Square. Hart was poetry editor of *Exodus* and author of several books of poetry. He lives in San Francisco.

Nat Hentoff writes about jazz, civil liberties, and education, and for over thirty-five years has been a staff writer for the *Village Voice*. Hentoff is also a syndicated columnist for the *Washington Post*. His latest books are *Free Speech for Me and Not for Thee* and *Listen to the Stories: Nat Hentoff on Jazz and Country Music*.

Sandra Hochman, born in New York, was educated at Bennington. She is a screenwriter, novelist, and playwright, and has written fiction for children. She lives and works in New York.

Ambrose J. Hollingworth appeared briefly in Beat coffee houses and was famous for his reading of his poem "Mental Toilet."

John Clellon Holmes, a leading spokesman for the Beat Generation, attended Columbia. He introduced the term "Beat Generation" in an essay in *New York Times Magazine* in 1952, the same year he published his first novel, *Go*. He won a Guggenheim fellowship in writing and established a creative writing program at the University of Arkansas. He died in 1988.

Dennis Hopper has been called a true 1960s character: He dressed like a Hell's Angel, mocked the establishment, attended rock concerts, smoked marijuana, hung out with New York artists, took photographs, and painted and sculpted. In his spare time, he acted in and directed the quintessential film of that era, *Easy Rider*. Since that time, Hopper has had a steady career in acting, directing, and producing movies.

Lita Hornick, born in New Jersey, studied at Barnard and Columbia University, where her doctoral dissertation was the first ever written on Dylan Thomas. In 1960, Hornick took over *Kulchur* magazine from Marc Schleifer. Hornick wrote books of criticism, including *Kulchur Queen*, *Night Flight*, and *Nine Martinis*; books of poetry; and a memoir, *The Green Fuse*.

Leonard Horowitz, who was born in Brooklyn and attended the Art Students League, was a popular figure at Beat parties, art openings, and in the coffee houses. He was an art and film critic for the *Village Voice* and the *Soho Weekly News*. He lived in the same lower Broadway loft for over twenty-five years, and was involved in avant-garde filmmaking, photography, and painting.

Harold (Doc) Humes, educated in science and chemical engineering at MIT and Harvard, was one of the founders and consulting editors of the *Paris Review*. When he lived in New York, he crusaded against police licensing of poetry readings in cafes and playing music in public parks, both criminal offenses in the 1950s. Humes is the author of *Underground City* and *Men Die*. His third novel, *Reflections on the Epitaph of Bernoule*, was never completed. He later lived in Cambridge, researching the physical and psychological problems of drug addiction and combat neurosis. He died in 1992.

Herbert Huncke, a legendary figure in the Beat movement, is Elmo Hassel in *On the Road*, Herman in *Junkie*, and Ancke in *Go*. Huncke met William Burroughs in the 1940s, around the time he acquired a habit for writing and for drugs, eventually spending five years in Sing Sing. In the 1950s, Huncke moved into Ginsberg's East 2nd Street building where he paid $30 a month for an apartment. He was first published in the newsletter, *Floating Bear*. A collection of autobiographic pieces, *The Evening Turned Crimson*, appeared in 1980; his memoir, *Guilty of Everything*, was published in 1987.

Angelo Ippolito, a painter and educator, was born in Italy but emigrated to the United States. He studied at the Ozenfant School of Fine Arts, the Brooklyn Museum Art School, and the Meschini Institute in Rome. His credits range from exhibits in Montreal, Sao Paulo, and Rotterdam to a Fulbright fellowship in Florence, Italy.

Ted Joans, born in Cairo, Ill., on a riverboat on the Fourth of July, is a jazz fanatic and surrealist painter, writer, poet, lecturer, and world traveler. His friendly presence was ubiquitous during the entire Beat era. He gave and went to more parties, poetry readings, and art openings than anyone else. He has at least twenty-nine books to his credit. He traveled to Africa and Europe in the early 1960s, and lived in Timbuktu. He now lives in New York, Seattle, and Paris. Joans was represented in the 1995 Whitney Museum Beat Generation exhibition.

Joyce Johnson, nee Glassman, met Kerouac through Allen Ginsberg, on a blind date at a Howard Johnson's restaurant in Greenwich Village in 1957. She and Kerouac became lovers, and she recounted the story of their relationship in her brilliant 1983 book *Minor Characters*. Johnson is a publishing executive and lives in New York.

Hettie Jones, nee Cohen, from Laurelton, Queens, N.Y., left home in 1951 for college and eventually hit Greenwich Village in 1956. She married LeRoi Jones in 1958, had two children, and was divorced in 1965. She worked on the *Partisan Review*, coedited *Yugen* and Totem Press Books with LeRoi Jones, and has written and edited numerous books for children, and her autobiography, *How I Became Hettie Jones* (1990).

LeRoi Jones became Imamu Amiri Baraka in the 1970s. He was educated at Rutgers, Howard University, and Columbia, served in the Air Force, and, with his then-wife Hettie Cohen, edited *Yugen* magazine and Totem Press books. Poet, musician, critic, essayist, dramatist, novelist, and political activist, Baraka first gained fame with the success of his play, *The Dutchman*, later made into a film by Shirley Clarke. *Transbluesncy: The Selected Poems of Amiri Baraka/LeRoi Jones (1961–1995)* offers a useful overview of his work. He has seven children and thirty books to his credit and lives and works in Newark, N.J., with his wife, Bidi Amina Baraka.

Matsumi Kanemitsu, born in Ogden, Utah, in 1922, grew up near Hiroshima. Returning to the United States in 1940, he enlisted in the U.S. Army. He studied painting with Yasuo Kuniyoshi at the Art Students League, and was identified with the New York School artists and writers that included Frank O'Hara. He died in 1992.

Howard Kanovitz is a painter who studied with Franz Kline, and also a talented jazz pianist. He has performed in a small jazz group that included Larry Rivers.

Bob Kaufman, born in New Orleans, spent 20 years in the U.S. merchant marine, which he joined at the age of 13. Known in France as the "Black American Rimbaud," he is the author of *Solitudes Crowded with Loneliness*, *The Golden Sardine*, and *The Ancient Rain*. He cofounded *Beatitude* magazine in 1959 with Allen Ginsberg, John Kelly, and Bill Margolis. Kaufman also acted in a couple of alternative films made in the late 1950s. In the 1960s, Kaufman took a Buddhist vow of silence, gave up writing, and withdrew into solitude. He died in 1986.

Jack Kerouac was born in Lowell, Mass. He attended the Horace Mann School in New York City in 1939 to prepare for entrance to Columbia University, where he had been awarded a football scholarship. Abandoning school after war was declared in 1941, he eventually joined the merchant marine, and later the U.S. Navy. Shortly after the war, he was introduced to William Burroughs and Allen Ginsberg by his first wife, Edie Parker, an artist. His first novel, *The Town and the City*, appeared in 1950. *On the Road* (1957), the defining novel of the Beat Generation, was his second published, and most famous and successful work. A prolific writer, he produced twenty-two volumes of fiction, poetry, and journals. During the 1960s, he suffered increasingly from anxiety and depression, worsened by alcoholism; he died in 1969.

Franz Kline, a leading figure in the abstract expressionist movement of the 1950s, was born in Wilkes-Barre, Pa. He studied art in Boston and London, came to New York in 1938, and had his first show in 1950. Teaching at Black Mountain College brought him in touch with numerous poets. Kline was the subject of writings by Frank O'Hara and Fielding Dawson, who wrote *An Emotional Memoir of Franz Kline*. Kline died in New York in 1962.

Kenneth Koch was born in Cincinnati, went to Harvard, and is a professor at Columbia University. Along with numerous volumes of poetry, Koch has published three books of plays, a novel, and several volumes about his experiences teaching children to write poetry. He has been both a Fulbright and a Guggenheim fellow and is a Bollingen prize winner.

Yaakov Kohn was editor of the irreverent tabloid weekly, *East Village Other*, and later the slightly more mainstream *Soho Weekly News*. Kohn, who had emigrated from Czechoslovakia to Israel, was a member of the Israeli underground, had a run-in with a British tank in 1948 that left him permanently disabled, and then came to the United States for medical treatment, where he became a gadfly journalist.

Sam Kramer owned a longtime Village jewelry studio at 29 West 8th Street, where he sold his own handcrafted, surrealistic jewelry. A flamboyant figure in Village lore, he was known as a judge of the annual Greenwich Village beauty queen contest, and for his lavish parties featuring flamenco dancers and mimes. At one event, on October 12, 1959, he masterminded a ceremony to cut away the plaster casts of Eddie Condon's broken arm and Anatole Broyard's broken leg.

Seymour Krim was a critic and writer whose anthology *The Beats* earned him a reputation as an authority. He taught at Columbia and lived in New York until his death in the 1980s.

Tuli Kupferberg, pamphleteer, poet, publisher of *Birth*, and author of over twenty books, in particular *1001 Ways to Beat the Draft*, *1001 Ways to Live Without Working*, and *1001 Ways to Make Love*, lives in Soho. He was a founder of the 1960s rad-rock group, the Fugs. Kupferberg is now a singing cartoonist and producer of "Revolting News" on cable TV. His latest book is *Teach Yourself Fucking*, and he is working on a musical comedy, *Marx in London*.

Philip Lamantia was identified as a surrealist poet by Andre Breton as early as 1943. He worked as an editor on *View*, the influential surrealist magazine of the 1940s headed by Charles Henri Ford. Later associated with the San Francisco Beat poets, Lamantia inspired the character of Francis Da Pavia in Kerouac's

Dharma Bums. Lamantia's works include *Erotic Poems, Ekstasis, Destroyed Works,* and *Becoming Visible.*

Cindy Lee (nee Amelia Maria-Theresa Laracuen) was a close friend of both Robert Graves and Howard Hart. She had been married to a professional diver, Owen Lee, and spent many summers in Deya, Majorca, where she met Graves. In 1961, she asked Graves for asylum after she stabbed her husband and left him for dead. Owen Lee survived, but the marriage did not. In 1962, she came to Deya with poet Howard Hart whom she had met in New York in 1959. When Graves came to New York on his lecture tours, Cindy Lee was frequently his escort.

Alfred Leslie, painter/film producer/anthologist, was born in New York and studied art at NYU. With Robert Frank, he coproduced the Beat film *Pull My Daisy.* In 1960 he compiled *The Hasty Papers*, an anthology of avant-garde art and writing. He was a Guggenheim fellow in 1969. A catastrophic fire in his loft on East 22nd Street destroyed all his early paintings. Leslie's paintings are in the Whitney and Museum of Modern Art collections.

Joseph LeSueur, a Californian, came to New York to study literature at Columbia University. An habitué of the downtown art scene, he lived with Frank O'Hara from 1955 until a year before O'Hara's untimely death in 1966. With Bill Berkson, he edited the highly regarded *Homage to Frank O'Hara.*

Denise Levertov, writer, teacher, poet, translator, was born in Ilford, Essex, England, worked as a nurse in London during World War II, and later married American writer Mitchell Goodman. Since 1946 she has published over twenty-five books of poems, essays, and translations. She is Fannie Hurst Professor at Brandeis University, a member of the American Academy and Institute of Arts and Letters, and a winner of the Elmer Holmes Bobst award in 1983.

Stephen Levine was born in New York. His first collection of poems, *A Resonance of Hope,* was published in 1959. He coedited the anthology *Writers in Revolt*, with Alex Trocchi, Terry Southern, and Richard Seaver.

Golda Lewis, an assemblage artist and papermaker, studied with Hans Hofmann and Jack Tworkov. Her work has been widely displayed, and she has taught hand papermaking. Lewis lives in New York.

Lawrence Lipton, poet, novelist, lecturer, and Beat chronicler, was born in Poland and died in Venice, Calif., in 1975 at the age of 76. He is best known for *The Erotic Revolution* and *The Holy Barbarians.* He also coauthored twenty-two books of mystery fiction under the pseudonym Craig Rice.

Daniel List, onetime U.S. Navy flight meteorologist, settled in Greenwich Village after the war, supporting himself by building picture frames and working in a coffee house. He was a sports car collector and repairman, which led to his writing career as auto columnist for the *Village Voice.* He also handled circulation for the *Voice* and later for the *Soho Weekly News* and the *New York Observer.*

Robert Losada is a lifelong New Yorker. He was an editor of *Odyssey Review*, a journal devoted to translations of writers not then widely known in English, was one of the founding editors of *The Annals of Scholarship*, an interdisciplinary journal in the humanities and social sciences. He recently retired from New York City's probation department, where he administered the intensive supervision program for the most serious offenders and a special program for juvenile felons.

Bob Lubin ran away from his Brooklyn home at the age of 16 to live the Bohemian life in Greenwich Village. He ran the poetry circle at the Gaslight Cafe in the 1950s, but gave up writing to follow his interest in carpentry and architectural design. Lubin lives in Soho.

Jimmy Lyons, born in California, followed his muse to Hollywood and New York. A singer, poet, and sound innovator, he works in a highly personal style. He combined his Beat poetry with expressionistic sounds, using saxophone, flute, piano and trumpet, bells, and percussion and electronic effects. Lyons lives in Oakland, Calif.

Michael C. D. Macdonald has worked in films, journalism, and politics. Son of the late Dwight Macdonald, author and critic, and Nancy Macdonald, who was honored by the Spanish government for her fundraising efforts on behalf of Spanish Civil War veterans (on the Republican side), Macdonald grew up in a milieu that included the foremost intellectuals of mid-20th century America. Macdonald wrote on political issues for the *Village Voice* in the 1960s and 1970s, and published *America's Cities: A Report on the Myth of Urban Renaissance* in 1984.

Norman Mailer, born in New Jersey and brought up in Brooklyn, was educated at Harvard. His first novel, *The Naked and the Dead*, published when he was 25 years old, was a Pulitzer prize winner and smashing success. Mailer was a cofounder in 1955 of the *Village Voice.* His classic 1957 essay, "The White Negro," was a brilliant study comparing hipsters to Negroes. Mailer has written over thirty books, ran for mayor of New York City, and was president of American PEN from 1984 to 1986. He lives in Brooklyn Heights.

Judith Malina, born in Kiel, Germany, is a director, actress, producer, and writer who cofounded the Living Theatre in New York with her late husband, Julian Beck. She has won numerous awards for her theatrical work, as well as international recognition for her work on behalf of the peace movement. Her writings include the futuristic play *Paradise Now, Poems of a Wandering Jewess,* and *The Diaries of Judith Malina.* Since Julian Beck's death, she has struggled to continue running the Living Theatre from a storefront in the East Village.

W. H. (Bill) Manville, magazine writer and novelist from Brooklyn, worked in an advertising agency before he went to the *Village Voice* to write the "Saloon Society" column, which later became the title of his first book. He wrote for *Cosmopolitan,* and is also the author of *Breaking Up, Goodbye,* and *The Palace of Money.*

Edward Marshall came from rural New Hampshire and attended New England College. He came to New York in 1953 to study religion and culture at Columbia. He published work in various Beat journals and in Donald Allen's anthology *The New American Poetry: 1945–1960,* in which Marshall's was the single longest poem. His three major works are *Hellan, Hellan; Transit Gloria;* and *Leave the Word Alone,* the last an epic outpouring about his mother.

Nancy Ward Martin and her twin sister, Joan Ward, came from Clarks Green, Pa., to New York after World War II. Nancy Ward studied at the Art Students League and became a commercial artist, handling department store accounts. A long-time companion to Franz Kline, she later married Peter D. Martin; her twin sister, Joan, was a long-time companion of painter Willem de Kooning. Nancy Martin died in 1973.

Peter D. Martin had a unique family history: His father was Carlo Tresca, editor of *Il Martello* (The Hammer) and the famous Italian anarchist, who was assassinated in 1943 on a New York City street corner. His mother, Sabina Flynn, was the youngest sister of Elizabeth Gurley Flynn, head of the American Communist Party. Martin's main interest was popular culture, although he sometimes said he was a Trotskyite. In San Francisco, he cofounded with Lawrence Ferlinghetti *City Lights* magazine and the related bookshop, but sold out his interest to Ferlinghetti early on to move to New York. After relocating, Martin worked at Bantam Books and married Nancy Ward. He died in 1988.

Michael McClure was born in Kansas, and in the early 1950s settled in San Francisco, where he became part of the Beat movement. He attended a writing workshop given by Robert Duncan and took part in a reading of Duncan's play *Faust Foutu* at the Six Gallery. McClure has written nine books of poetry and twenty plays, including *Scratching the Beat Surface* in 1982.

David McReynolds, a native of Los Angeles, graduated with a degree from UCLA in political science, was a Socialist Party candidate for president in 1980, and has written extensively on politics, art, culture, and the history of the pacifist movement. He currently works full-time for the War Resisters League in New York. His essays are collected in *We Have Been Invaded by the 21st Century.*

Taylor Mead was born in Detroit, the son of a powerful politician. He is better known for his comic acting roles than his literary accomplishments. The star of Andy Warhol's 1968 film *Lonesome Cowboy*, Mead also played in Ron Rice's *Flower Thief* and *Queen of Sheba Meets the Atom Man*, and Jonas Mekas's *Hallelujah the Hills* and *Babo 73*. He won an Obie award for his performance in Frank O'Hara's play *The General Returns from One Place to Another*. Mead's poetry notebooks have been published as *Excerpts from the Anonymous Diary* of *a New York Youth*. He lives in New York.

Jonas Mekas was a film critic for the *Village Voice* who became known as the guru of underground film. He filmed the Living Theatre's production of Kenneth Brown's *The Brig*, which won the grand prize of the Venice Documentary Film Festival in 1964. Mekas founded the Filmmakers Cinematheque on Second Avenue, as well as the Anthology Film Archives.

David Meltzer is a New York-born poet identified with the Beat movement. His home base is now San Francisco. He has written poetry, experimental fiction with erotic themes, and *We All Have Something to Say to Each Other*, which includes an essay on Kenneth Patchen and four poems.

Jack Micheline, Bronx-born author and playwright, has ten volumes to his credit. Micheline is well-established in the Bohemian tradition as a street poet-balladeer. He lives in San Francisco.

Gilbert Millstein, an editor at the *New York Times Sunday Magazine* in 1952, assigned John Clellon Holmes to write the article "This Is the Beat Generation"; it was the first article on the subject. On September 5, 1957, Millstein wrote the first important review of *On the Road*; it appeared in the *Times*, where he was a staff writer. Millstein was an early organizer of jazz and poetry readings that featured Kerouac.

Charles Mingus, born in Nogales, Ariz., was a premier composer and bass player, and an early performer of jazz with poetry. He won Guggenheim fellowships in 1971 and 1978. His autobiography, *Beneath the Underdog*, appeared in 1971; he died in 1979, leaving behind 300 compositions, many of them unrecorded and never performed.

Joan Mitchell, a prominent painter of the New York School, studied at Smith College and the Art Institute of Chicago. The Chicago-born artist moved to France in the 1960s, where she continued to work until her death in 1992. A major retrospective of her life and work was presented at the Jeu de Paume in Paris in 1994.

John Mitchell managed the Gaslight Cafe on MacDougal Street; it was the liveliest coffee house in Greenwich Village in the 1950s, and many Beat poets read there. He joined forces with other club owners and local politicians to pressure City Hall to permit cafes to hold poetry readings without having to obtain a cabaret license. As fashions in entertainment changed, the cafe first featured folk music, and then stand-up comics to bring in customers. Mitchell published an anthology of Beat Generation poets, *Gaslight Poetry Review*.

Barbara Moraff went to Columbia and had her first book, *Four Young Lady Poets*, published by Corinth Press in 1962. She has published several other poetry collections, and excerpts from her journals. Moraff lives in Vermont, where she works as a potter and cofounded a crafts school.

William Morris, born Wolfe Zolkwer in Glasgow, Scotland, was a pupil of poet William Carlos Williams and artist Joan Miro. One of the most visible of MacDougal Street coffee house poets, Morris was also an accomplished artist who once had an exhibit consisting of paintings created by using a truck tire instead of a paintbrush. His antics were often reported in the media. Morris moved to England in the early 1960s and went to sea as a merchant seaman. A back injury necessitated an operation that went badly, causing him to spend his last years in a wheelchair. He died in London in 1996.

Dody Müller, widow of the painter Jan Müller, is a creative and independent artist in her own right and has exhibited often. One of Jack Kerouac's many girlfriends, Müller gave him painting lessons. Dennis McNally, in his biography of Kerouac, *Desolate Angel*, describes her as "an exciting vibrant woman, a hard-drinking rocker with long, beautiful dark hair, a husky sensual voice and a tremendous laugh." Kerouac's mother, on the other hand, accused her of taking her son away.

Brigid Murnaghan, born in the "Holyland of the Bronx," moved to MacDougal Street in Greenwich Village in 1948, and by 1984 had moved one block away to Bleecker Street. She was the first film critic for the *Village Voice*, where her terse, lucid, incisive reviews earned her a wide reputation. She has been a central figure on the Village scene for many decades, writing and reading her poetry, and running a weekly salon in a Bleecker Street tavern. Her latest book of poems is *Out of the Drawer of Brigid Murnaghan*.

Anaïs Nin, the legendary novelist and diarist, was born in Paris and arrived in the United States as a teenager. She achieved fame with the publication of *The Diary of Anaïs Nin 1931–1966*, a chronicle of avant-garde life in Paris and New York. One of her major diary themes was the establishment and psychological acceptance of a feminine identity. Nin died in 1977.

Eric Nord, whose real name was Harry Hilmuth Pastor, first opened a coffee house in Venice, Calif., that he called the Gas House, where, as *Time* magazine said in 1959, "the jukebox blared the beatniks' 3 B's: Bach, Bartók and Bird." Nord's famed "party pad" was an old produce warehouse where he threw bottle parties and poetry readings, and charged $1 admission. Nord's eccentricities, scrapes with the police, and defense of the Beats made him the high priest of the San Francisco scene. He eventually became the entrepreneur of North Beach's historic Beat rendezvous, the Co-Existence Bagel Shop.

Frank O'Hara, art critic and poet, was born in Baltimore, raised in New England, and educated at Harvard. He was a curator at the Museum of Modern Art from 1951 until his sudden death on July 25, 1966, when he was struck by a Fire Island beach taxi. O'Hara was a founder of the New York School of Poetry, a clique of mostly non-Beat Harvard poets and second-generation abstract painters. He produced fourteen books and is eulogized in *Homage to Frank O'Hara*, edited by Bill Berkson and Joseph LeSueur.

Joel Oppenheimer came from Yonkers, N.Y., was educated at Cornell, the University of Chicago, and Black Mountain College, and was an accomplished poet, novelist, and playwright as well as a sports writer (*The Wrong Season*). He was a columnist for the *Village Voice* for many years and resident poet at City College. Oppenheimer left New York to teach journalism and creative writing at New England College. He died in 1988.

Peter Orlovsky posed nude with Allen Ginsberg for a full-length photograph by Richard Avedon in 1963. Circulated widely as a poster, the image helped raise public awareness of gay unions. The poets met in 1954 in North Beach. Three years later, while in Paris, Orlovsky began to write poetry. Traveling with Ginsberg in India in 1961, Orlovsky encountered a beggar woman dying of leprosy on a street in Benares; this experience resulted in a poem, "Lepers Cry." His *Straight Hearts Delight: Love Poems and Selected Letters* was published in 1980.

Grace Paley, writer, political activist, and teacher, lives in Vermont. A long-time faculty member of Sarah Lawrence College, she devoted much effort in the 1960s and 1970s to the peace movement and counseling young people of draft age. In 1994, Paley published her *Collected Stories*.

Kenneth Patchen, who died at the age of 60 in 1972, was an elder statesman to the San Francisco Beats. In the 1950s, he launched a new image of the poet as a hip public figure by combining poetry with jazz in performances in nightclubs, concert halls, and on radio and TV. In addition to publishing more than two dozen books, Patchen made several records of his readings with jazz accompaniment.

George A. Plimpton, wrestler, baseball player, prizefighter, and noted editor of the *Paris Review*, was born and lives in New York. His books, many of which recount his assuming the role of a professional athlete, include *Paper Lion*, *One for the Record*, and *The X-Factor*.

Larry Poons was born in Ogikubo, near Tokyo, Japan. He attended the New England Conservatory of Music, but became a painter. Poons moved to New York and took a Front Street loft in 1958. He ran the Epitome, 165 Bleecker Street, one of the lively poetry cafes of the Beat era. Poons's art has been shown in galleries and museums worldwide.

George Nelson Preston ran the storefront "Artist's Studio" at 48 East 3rd Street where he presented many important poetry readings in the late 1950s. He is now a professor of art history at CUNY, specializing in African art.

Henry Proach played more than fifteen roles in Living Theatre productions after joining the company in 1951. He is best remembered as the spastic in *The Apple* and as Harry in *The Connection*, a role he repeated in the film version.

Dan Propper graduated from P.S. 18 in Brooklyn. He received recognition as a poet with "The Fable of the Final Hour," published in Seymour Krim's *The Beats*. Propper participated in jazz readings with Dizzy Gillespie and Thelonious Monk. His book *For Kerouac in Heaven* was published in 1980. Propper lives in Woodstock, N.Y.

Margaret Randall was a central figure on the New York Beat scene. She moved to Mexico City in 1961, where she edited *El Corno Emplumado* for eight years. She spent twenty-three years outside the United States, living in Mexico, Cuba, and Nicaragua. She returned in 1984 and settled in Albuquerque, N. M., where she works as a poet, oral historian, and photographer. Among her twenty-some books are *Christians in the Nicaraguan Revolution*; *Spirit of the People: The Women of Vietnam*; and *Sandino's Daughters*.

Jerome Raphel began his acting career with the Living Theatre, appearing in *Many Loves*, *The Connection*, *The Cave at Machpelah*, and *Tonight We Improvise*. He has appeared in several television dramas and the film version of *The Connection*. He also played in LeRoi Jones's *The Slave* at the St. Marks Playhouse.

Marc Ratliff moved to New York in 1955 to attend Cooper Union. One of the founders of the avant-garde Judson Gallery, he also was a founder and the art editor of the Beat magazine *Exodus*. Jim Dine, a hometown chum; Claes Oldenburg, who worked in the Cooper Union library; and Tom Wesselmann were discovered by Ratliff and had their first shows at the Judson.

Kenneth Rexroth, anarchist, poet, painter, dramatist, critic, translator, editor, and mentor of the San Francisco Beats, died in 1982 at the age of 76. He had been West Coast literary correspondent for *The Nation* and *Saturday Review*. Winner of numerous awards, including a 1948 Guggenheim fellowship, Rexroth organized the famous poetry reading at the Six Gallery, a former auto-repair shop on Fillmore Street, in San Francisco, on October 7, 1955, which launched the West Coast Beat movement.

Larry Rivers, poet, painter, and saxophone player, originally sought his fortune as a musician. Intrigued by the intellectual aspects of painting, he became instead a critically acclaimed painter, one of the few successful figurative artists in the heyday of abstract expressionism. He read poetry at the Living Theatre and portrayed Milo, the Neal Cassady character, in Robert Frank's film *Pull My Daisy*. He collaborated with Frank O'Hara in combining visual images with poetry, and designed stage sets for O'Hara, Kenneth Koch, and LeRoi Jones. With playwright Arnold Weinstein, Rivers wrote a memoir, *What Did I Do? The Unauthorized Autobiography of Larry Rivers* (1992). He lives in Southampton, N.Y.

Cynthia Robinson graduated from Sarah Lawrence and received a scholarship to study at the American Shakespeare Festival Theatre in Stratford. Her first off-Broadway appearance, at the Living Theatre, was in the 1959 premiere of William Carlos Williams's *Many Loves*.

Hugh Romney was a dapper figure among the younger Beat poets in Greenwich Village in the late 1950s. In one of his memorable readings, he teamed up with the blind musician Moondog and falsetto singer Tiny Tim, the trio performing at the Fat Black Pussy Cat at 13 Minetta Street. Romney was an organizer of the 1968 "Pigasus for President" election campaign, and emceed at the Woodstock Music Festival the following year. By then, Romney had assumed the persona of "Wavy Gravy," nonsense guru of the Hog Farm, a traveling commune. An anti-Vietnam war activist, Romney was the star of Robert Frank's film *Life-Raft-Earth*. Romney lives in Berkeley and leads a circus called *Camp Winnarainbow*.

Harold Rosenberg wrote the landmark article "The American Action Painters," for *Art News*, December 1952, and was an early champion of Abstract Expressionism. His phrase "action painting" was picked up by other critics and the public to describe the work process of artists such as Jackson Pollock. Rosenberg was art editor for the acclaimed WPA American Guide series (1938-1940). His own books included *Art on the Edge* and *Willem de Kooning*. Rosenberg was art critic at *The New Yorker* from 1962 until his death in 1978.

Irving Rosenthal was a controversial editor who first published two excerpts from William Burroughs's *Naked Lunch* when he was editing *The Chicago Review*, and later founded the journal *Big Table*.

Barney Rosset, founder and editor of Grove Press, was publisher and editor, along with Fred Jordan, Richard Seaver, and Donald Allen, of *Evergreen Review*, the most influential of Beat era periodicals. Over ninety-five issues were published between 1957 and 1967, containing the work of avant-garde writers, poets, playwrights, composers, painters, and photographers. After selling Grove Press in the mid-1980s, Rosset has continued to work in publishing.

Albert Saijo, a minister's son, was born in Los Angeles. At the age of fifteen, he was interned at Heart Mountain Camp during World War II, when the U.S. government considered anyone of Japanese descent a security threat. Saijo moved to North Beach in the mid-1950s, where he met Lew Welch, Philip Whalen, and Gary Snyder. In 1959, Welch introduced Saijo to Kerouac, and the three friends set off on a cross-country trip to New York, composing haiku to entertain themselves on the way. The haikus were later incorporated into a book, called *Trip Trap*, and also inspired the poem composed by Kerouac, Saijo, and Welch for McDarrah's anthology, *The Beat Scene*.

Irving H. Sandler, writer, critic, and teacher, published the definitive book on the New York School, *The Triumph of American Painting: A History of Abstract Expressionism* (1970). He has taught at NYU and is a professor at the State University of New York at Purchase.

William Saroyan was a noted author of stories, novels, and plays, including the Pulitzer prize winning *The Time of Your Life*. Saroyan's writings, especially those about small towns, were a major influence on Jack Kerouac. The style of Kerouac's first full-length work, *Atop an Underwood*, bears many traces of Saroyan, Ernest Hemingway, and Thomas Wolfe.

Marc D. Schleifer was the founder and editor of *Kulchur*, which was supported by Lita Hornick. After the first three issues appeared, Schleifer went to Cuba. One of the early contributors to the *Village Voice*, he converted from Judaism to the Muslim faith, changing his name to Suleiman Abdullah Schleifer. He moved to Cairo, Egypt, where he worked for NBC News and taught at the American University.

Abram Schlemowitz, New York-born artist and teacher, used bronze and steel to make abstract sculptures. He taught at Pratt Institute and Kingsborough College. A Guggenheim fellow, he also won awards from the Longview and Gottlieb foundations, and displayed his work widely.

James Schuyler was one of the New York School of poets, a group associated with Frank O'Hara. He won the 1981 Pulitzer prize for *The Morning of the Poem*. He was a Guggenheim fellow, fellow of the American Academy of Poets, critic for *Art News*, and a staff member of the Museum of Modern Art. He died in 1991.

Delmore Schwartz was born in Brooklyn in 1913. He studied philosophy at the University of Wisconsin, New York University, and Harvard. In 1938, his first volume of poetry, *In Dreams Begin Responsibilities*, was hailed by critics. He went on to write lyrics, fiction, drama, and criticism, and was an editor of *Partisan Review* and also the *New Republic*. He won the Bollingen prize in 1960. His early success was followed by a tragic descent into alcoholism and mental illness; Schwartz died in 1966.

Anne Wedgwood-Schwertley came to New York in 1956. She took classes at the Art Students League and the New School, and was codirector of the Fine Arts Conservation Laboratories. She formed a close relationship with painter Franz Kline, but after he died she moved away from the scene.

Richard Seaver edited the literary magazine *Merlin* in 1950s Paris, publishing early works by Samuel Beckett, Jean Genet, and Eugene Ionesco. In the 1960s, he moved to New York and was managing editor of *Evergreen Review* and editorial director of Grove Press. With his wife, Jeannette, he founded Seaver Books, an imprint of Viking Press. The Seavers now manage Arcade Publishing, a small house whose books are distributed by Little, Brown.

Hubert Selby, Jr., was born and raised in Brooklyn. He went to sea as a merchant marine for several years before contracting tuberculosis in Germany and spending three years in the hospital. After his release, he returned to the states seeking a career as a writer. To support himself, he worked as a clerk, secretary, and typist. His most famous work is the controversial novel *Last Exit to Brooklyn* (Grove Press, 1960), which was made into a Hollywood movie.

Peter H. Selz studied at the University of Chicago and the University of Paris. He was chief curator of painting and sculpture at the Museum of Modern Art from 1958 to 1965, noted for his support of avant-garde art. He is a senior fellow of the National Endowment for the Humanities.

Shel Silverstein, author, cartoonist, composer, and folksinger, was a correspondent for *Pacific Stars and Stripes*, and achieved fame and fortune as a regular contributor to *Playboy* magazine. He has written and illustrated many children's books, and created the famous Uncle Shelby character.

Howard Smith was 20 years old in 1957 when his first article, describing Kerouac's reading poetry at the Village Vanguard, appeared in the *Village Voice*. His "Scenes" column began appearing in the paper in 1966. Smith has had a wide-ranging career, as a magazine writer, photojournalist, nationally syndicated radio talk-show host, and cable television programming consultant. He also produced and directed *Gizmo* and the Academy Award-winning film, *Marjoe*. Smith lives in New York.

William Lloyd Smith was a Chicago Beatnik philosopher who ran for president in 1960. As a "pacifist anarchist," he wanted to abolish the government and return the United States to a group of primitive tribes. His campaign, although widely publicized, gained little support. He was an ideal oddball candidate, one who couldn't and didn't even want to win, and in fact disapproved on principle of winning. His campaign manager, Slim Brundage, was owner of the West 10th Street bar, the College of Complexes.

Robert Smithson, who studied at the Art Students League and the Brooklyn Museum, was an innovative figure in the early days of minimal art. He was later best-known for rearranging landscapes with earth-moving equipment, resulting in works that were monumental in scale, and subject to the natural forces of temperature, weather, and erosion. Smithson died in a plane crash in 1973 while viewing one of his earthworks in Texas.

Gary Snyder, lumberjack, linguist, anthropologist, and poet, was born in San Francisco, graduated from Reed College, and studied classical Chinese at Cal.-Berkeley. In 1956, he went to live in a Japanese monastery and study Zen Buddhism. He inspired the character of Japhy Ryder in Kerouac's *Dharma Bums*. He published his first book, *Riprap*, in 1959, and has since won Bollingen and Guggenheim fellowships and a Pulitzer Prize in 1974 for his book *Turtle Island*.

Harriet Sohmers, writer, editor, and translator, lived in Paris for ten years, where she worked for the *International Herald Tribune*. Her writing has appeared in both avant-garde and popular magazines; she also edited the *Provincetown Review*.

Carl Solomon, born in the Bronx, was a child prodigy. He attended Brooklyn College and the Sorbonne. When he turned 21, he voluntarily committed himself into the Psychiatric Institute in New York for shock therapy to treat his severe depression. Allen Ginsberg, who met Solomon in 1949, immortalized his friend by dedicating "Howl" to him. Solomon later became an editor at Ace Books, a publishing company owned by his uncle. Solomon published William Burroughs's first book, *Junkie*, and paid Kerouac a $250 advance for *On the Road*, although Ace never published the book.

Susan Sontag earned a master's degree in philosophy from Harvard and began writing fiction and criticism in her late twenties, and has become one of the most influential cultural critics in the United States. Her writings include *Notes on Camp*, *Styles of Radical Will*, *Illness as Metaphor*, and *On Photography*.

Gilbert Sorrentino lived in Brooklyn when he edited and published *Neon* from 1956 to 1960. He also worked as an editor at Grove Press. Sorrentino has written poetry, short stories, and novels. He taught at the New School and became a full professor at Stanford University in Palo Alto, Calif.

Terry Southern was a Texas-born writer of novels and screenplays. He achieved notoriety in 1958 with the publication of his novel *Candy*. Southern's best-known screenwriting credits include *Easy Rider* (with Peter Fonda and Dennis Hopper), *Dr. Strangelove* (with Stanley Kubrick), and *The Loved One* (with Christopher Isherwood). Southern died in 1995.

Patsy Southgate, a native New Yorker, graduated from Smith College with a B.A. in French literature. She lived in Paris, working as a translator and contributing articles to the *Paris Review*. Back in the United States, Southgate continued writing short stories, plays, and poems that were published in *Evergreen Review*. She currently lives in East Hampton.

William Styron's best-known works are the Pulitzer prize novel *Confessions of Nat Turner* and *Sophie's Choice*, which was also an Oscar-winning film. Styron has been an editor at the *Paris Review* since 1953 and is on the editorial board of *American Scholar*.

Mark Sufrin is the author of biographies of Woodrow Wilson, Stephen Crane, F. Scott Fitzgerald, and Walt Whitman, among other notable political and literary figures. He has published articles on film and social and literary history, as well as short stories and essays. He was the writer and a codirector of the prize-winning film, *On the Bowery*.

May Swenson was a poet born and educated in Utah. Her first published work, "Another Animal: Poems" (1954), appearing in *Poets of Today I*, was acclaimed for its vivid imagery and experimental typography and technique. She was the recipient of a MacArthur Foundation fellowship and a co-winner of the Bollingen prize. She died in 1989.

Jerry Tallmer, a founding member of the *Village Voice* staff, was associate editor and drama critic. Under his direction, the *Voice* covered off-Broadway theater and began the Obie awards. Tallmer was a reporter and cultural critic for the *New York Post* from 1962 to 1991. He was one of the first writers to interview Kerouac after *On the Road* was published.

Sylvia Topp, who lives in Soho, has written for the *North American Review*, *Village Voice*, and *Birth* magazine. She was production manager for *Soho Weekly News* and currently holds that position at the *Voice*. She edited a series of books on the early writing, art, and photographs of well-known people as children.

Gloria Tropp was born in Mount Vernon, N.Y. In the early 1950s, she moved to the East Village, and made the downtown scene at the Waldorf Cafeteria, San Remo, and the Open Door jazz club, where she sang ballads and bebop. With her husband, Stephen Tropp, she performed jazz and poetry in coffee houses. Since his death, she has performed with the ensemble Talking Free Be-bop. She is also featured on the nationally televised "Women in Limbo" art forum.

Stanley Twardowicz, painter and photographer, was Kerouac's neighbor in Northport, Long Island, where Kerouac lived with his mother in 1962. The painter and the writer became close friends; Kerouac was the only person

Twardowicz permitted in his studio. Twardowicz received a Guggenheim fellowship in 1955, and his work is in the collections of many major museums.

Kenneth Tynan, the British drama critic, took a highly partisan role as a critic. His acerbic reviews first ran in the *London Evening Standard*, then in the *Observer*, and in 1958 he became drama critic of the *New Yorker*. His play, *O! Calcutta!* (1969) created a public debate on morality in the theater. Ill with emphysema, he moved to Los Angeles in 1976, where he died fourteen years later at the age of 53.

Gore Vidal, novelist and essayist, was born at West Point, N.Y., where his father was an aeronautics instructor. Gore began to write when he was in preparatory school, and finished his first novel, *Williwaw* (1946), when he was just 19. His third novel, *The City and the Pillar* (1948), an account of a young man's coming to terms with his homosexuality, brought him national recognition. He has written several historical novels; the best-known are *Burr* (1973) and *Lincoln* (1984). His memoir, *Palimpsest*, appeared in 1995. Vidal lives in Italy.

Jose Garcia Villa, a native of the Philippines, was editor of *Wake* in the 1940s and taught poetry at the New School for Social Research. He was an adviser to the Philippine government on cultural affairs. His poetry has been collected in *The Portable Villa* and *The Essential Villa*.

Ronald Von Ehmsen represented the media version of a bearded Beat poet. He modeled for fashion magazines, rented himself out as a Beat personality, and ran the Cafe Rafio at 165 Bleecker Street. One day, wanting to enlarge the cafe, he served an eviction notice to the tenant in the rear of the building. The angry 73-year-old occupant pulled out a .32 caliber revolver and shot Von Ehmsen three times, killing him in the middle of Bleecker Street.

William V. Ward, a native New Yorker, lived in Paris and also spent two years in India on a research project. A poet himself, he was editor of the *Provincetown Review*. Ward lives in Brooklyn Heights and worked for the New York City Board of Education.

Vincent Warren and Frank O'Hara met on August 10, 1959, and became good friends. Warren was a ballet dancer who had performed for two years in the Metropolitan Opera Ballet Company; he also worked with the modern dance choreographer James Waring. Warren inspired O'Hara to write openly gay love poems, which led to O'Hara's being identified, after his death, as an early poet of the Gay Liberation movement.

Lew Welch was a high-school track star who enjoyed reading Joyce Kilmer and Robert Service. At Reed College, he roomed wih Philip Whalen and Gary Snyder. Welch, Kerouac, and Albert Saijo collaborated on the 1959 collection *Trip Trap, Haiku Along the Road from San Francisco to New York*. Welch's collected works appeared in 1977, five years after his strange disappearance in the foothills of the Sierra Nevada, described in Aram Saroyan's definitive portrait, *Genesis Angels* (Morrow, 1977).

Philip Whalen, now an ordained Zen priest, was born in Oregon and attended Reed College where he shared a room with Gary Snyder and Lew Welch. A leading figure of the San Francisco poetry renaissance, he first gained notoriety by reading at the Six Gallery on October 13, 1955. He has published over twenty books, including *Memoirs of an Interglacial Age* and *On Bear's Head: Selected Poems*.

John Wieners graduated from Boston College and attended Black Mountain College. Wieners moved into the Hotel Wentley, in San Francisco, and took a job sweeping floors at the Coffee Gallery, a Beat hangout in North Beach. Wieners founded the magazine *Measure*, which published poets associated with Black Mountain and with the San Francisco Beat movement. He is the author of the dime-store opus *She'd Turn on a Dime*, *The Hotel Wentley Poems*, *Behind the State Capitol*, and *Delores*.

John Wilcock, English-born writer, was a newspaper reporter in London. A founding contributor to the *Village Voice*, he wrote a column, "Village Square," that ran for over ten

years. He also wrote for a competing underground paper, *East Village Other*. He moved to the West Coast, where he edits and writes travel books.

Eli Wilentz, who died in 1995, co-owned, with his brother Ted, the famous 8th Street Bookshop.

Ted Wilentz was co-owner (with his brother, Eli) of the 8th Street Bookshop, a noted literary meeting place in Greenwich Village. Wilentz and his family lived above the store and welcomed writers and artists at informal gatherings. The brothers quarreled and Ted left the bookstore in 1968. The store suffered a disastrous fire in 1976 and closed three years later. Corinth Books, a small press that produced many books by Beat-era writers and poets, was an outgrowth of the shop; Ted continued to run the imprint for a while after leaving the bookstore. Wilentz now lives in Maryland.

Jonathan C. Williams, poet, publisher, essayist, photographer, and hiker, was born in Asheville, N.C., and educated at Princeton, and Black Mountain College. He is best-known for publishing Jargon Society books, which include important texts by Charles Olson, Robert Duncan, Louis Zukofsky, Kenneth Patchen, and Mina Loy. Williams has won a Guggenheim fellowship and a grant from the National Endowment for the Arts.

Daniel Wolf, cofounder and first editor of the *Village Voice*, studied at the New School for Social Research and started his writing career at the *Columbia Encyclopedia*. In 1955, along with Norman Mailer and Edwin Fancher, he founded the newspaper that championed the liberal cause in politics and new-wave art. After the original owners sold the *Voice*, Wolf became an adviser to then-mayor Edward Koch. Wolf died in 1996.

Marian Zazeela studied painting at Bennington College. She has presented light installations and conducted light performances in the United States and Europe, and won NEA and CAPS grants. She often collaborates with avant-garde composer LaMonte Young (her husband), and has been studying Indian classical vocal music with Pandit Pran Nath.

Louis Zukofsky was born in New York City in 1904 of Russian immigrant parents. He began writing lyric poetry as a young man, but his first volume was not published until 1965, *All the Collected Short Poems, 1923–1958*. His best-known work, the poem *A*, was written in installments from 1928 to 1979, and had many historical and personal themes. Zukofsky died in 1978.

index

Entries that appear in bold type refer to photographs.

theauthors

Fred W. McDarrah, born in Brooklyn, made an early and important contribution to Beat literature with his photos and the poems he collected for *The Beat Scene* (1960). His anthology *Kerouac and Friends* was published in 1985. He has won a Guggenheim Fellowship in photography as well as Page One awards from the Newspaper Guild of New York for spot news photography. McDarrah's work was shown in the Beat Generation exhibits at the Whitney Museum in 1995 and at the National Portrait Gallery of the Smithsonian in 1996. He has been picture editor for the *Village Voice* for over 35 years.

Gloria Schoffel McDarrah, born in the Bronx, is a literary critic, editor, and travel writer. She contributed to the editorial development of *The Beat Scene* and coauthored *The Artist's World* and *Museums in New York*. McDarrah has written travel guides to destinations in the United States and abroad. When not traveling, she lives in New York.